A Woman's Guide to Spiritual Wellness
A Personal Study of Colossians

TABLE OF CONTENTS

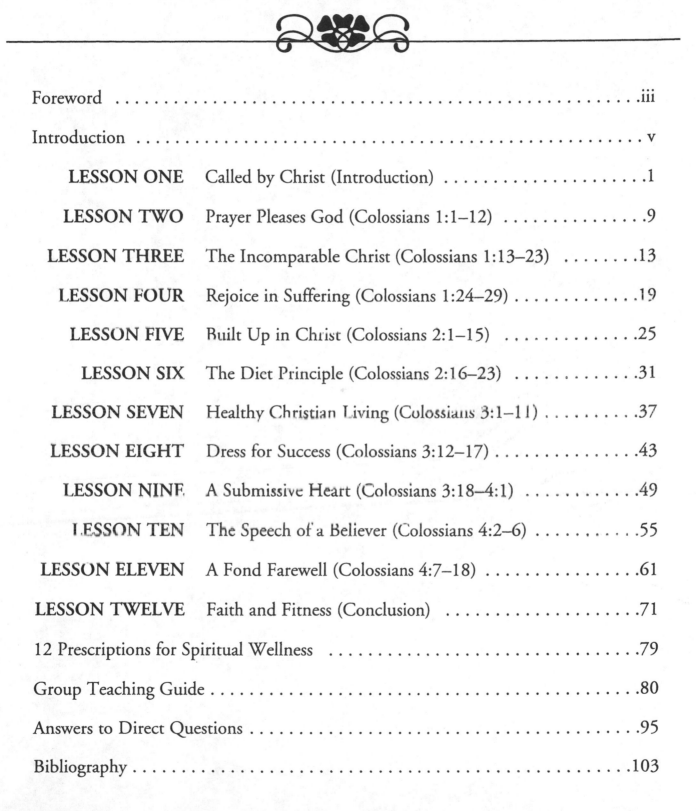

FOREWORD

*O*n a daily basis, I work diligently to take care of my physical condition. I discipline myself to walk three miles at least three days a week. I try to eat a nutritious diet. I see my doctor annually for a complete physical examination. And I even attempt to get proper rest. I have been taught to take care of my body, to prevent physical illness. Wellness is important to my personal life and to my ministry.

It is important for me as a Christian to be just as conscientious about spiritual wellness as I am about my physical condition. Rather than waiting for spiritual illness to occur, I work faithfully on my personal spiritual growth. Prayer, Bible study, service, and witnessing are essential prescriptions for my spiritual wellness. When I falter in building my relationship with the Lord, my spiritual condition weakens and I become susceptible to sin. The book of Colossians has become a prescriptive medication for my own spiritual wellness. Paul's insights into Christian living have strengthened my spiritual stamina and helped me resist illness.

Walk with me through this study of the book of Colossians and discover the care of the Great Physician!

—Rhonda Harrington Kelley

INTRODUCTION

This Bible study contains twelve lessons which thoroughly examine God's guidelines for spiritual wellness from the book of Colossians. Several tools are necessary before you begin your personal study. First, you must make a genuine commitment to complete the study you begin. You may desire to spend time in God's Word, but you must discipline yourself to do it. Try to read through the book of Colossians several times during your study.

Next, you should select a Bible translation that is readable and has features you prefer. (This Bible study uses the New King James Version unless otherwise noted.) You may also find it helpful to read certain passages in several translations to gain additional insights. And don't hesitate to underline or write in your Bible as you begin your personal study.

Each lesson is designed to focus on one passage of Scripture, though the approach to each study varies. Some lessons are verse-by-verse studies, while others deal with the theme of the overall passage. However, each lesson encourages personal response and includes a Scripture focus ("Prescription for Spiritual Wellness") and practical application ("Personal Spiritual Wellness"). The selected key Scripture is excellent for Bible memory. Store up these biblical truths and apply them in your daily life.

This Bible study was written for individual study. Read the Scripture and complete the study questions personally. Begin your Bible study time with prayer. Ask God to speak to you clearly, reveal Himself plainly, and increase your knowledge of His Word continually. After you pray, read the focal passage of Scripture. Reading aloud is often helpful. Take time to hear the Word, as well as see it. Answer the questions as they are asked. Each lesson should take you from 30 to 45 minutes to complete. The study is designed to last twelve weeks, with one lesson per week. Don't hurry through the study; instead, let each biblical truth become real to you.

You may also share this study of the book of Colossians with a small group. Each person should complete their own study and then discuss it with the group. A group leader should facilitate the discussion and organize the group. One-hour sessions are suggested. Interaction with others about the book of Colossians will enhance your learning experience and promote your spiritual growth. In addition, group participation will hold you accountable. (See the Group Teaching Guide on page 81 for suggestions about leading a small group Bible study.)

When you have completed your study of Colossians, share what you have learned with someone else and apply what God has taught you in your daily life. Bible study should make a difference in your life and in the lives of others. You will be strengthened spiritually, and you will promote spiritual wellness in your own life. May God richly bless your Bible study.

Physicians today are focusing medical interventions more on prevention than on treatment. Most prefer physical wellness for the body over the treatment of illness. Believers should challenge themselves to seek spiritual wellness for the soul. Wellness involves the total person. Therefore, individuals should care for themselves physically, spiritually, emotionally, and mentally. Women are particularly challenged to juggle the many demands of their busy lives so they can nurture their families and manage their responsibilities.

The book of Colossians contains many theological truths and doctrinal statements, but it can also be used as a practical guide for women moving toward a lifestyle of spiritual wellness. Paul, himself, gave instruction and encouragement to his Christian friends in Colosse who were facing spiritual challenges. His inspired words from God became a prescription for spiritual wellness and can guide Christians today. This study is designed to help you better understand the biblical teachings of Colossians and to apply those godly principles in your lives today.

My prayer is for you to become healthier as you dig into the Word of God, and for you to develop a lifestyle of wellness that will strengthen and sustain you for the rest of your life. As we begin our journey toward spiritual wellness, let's investigate the background of the book of Colossians.

THE AUTHOR

The New Testament letter of Colossians was undoubtedly written by the apostle Paul. Though he apparently had not visited the city or founded the church there, he had personal interest in the Christians at Colosse (Col. 2:1).

Who wrote the book of Colossians? _Apostle Paul_____

Who was with him?_____

Had Paul visited Colosse? _____No_____

What phrase supports your answer? _____

In recent history, some biblical scholars have questioned the authorship of this letter primarily for three reasons:

1. Some say that the book of Colossians contains words and phrases not typical of Paul's other writings.
2. Some say that gnostic thought, which is a prominent subject in the book of Colossians, did not develop until a much later time than that of Paul.
3. The view of Christ recorded in Colossians is more advanced than any other of Paul's discussions of Christ.

Most scholars today accept Paul's authorship of Colossians. He identified himself as author in verse one; he expressed himself in different ways by the inspiration of God; he definitely encountered the roots of gnostic thinking; and over time and through new experiences, he developed his understanding of Christ.

What do you know about the man Paul? _He was once named Paul and he prescuted Christians. On the way to Damasus he was blinded & then transformed into a believer of CHRIST. From that point on he preached the Gospel of Jesus CHRIST_

Saul was born in Tarsus (Acts 22:3), a bustling city in southern Turkey, in approximately A.D. 1–5. Scripture records that he was born a Jew, raised strictly as a Jew, and served faithfully as a Jewish leader. In fact, Saul became known as "a Hebrew of the Hebrews" (Phil. 3:5) because of his adherence to Old Testament laws and traditions and his scholarly training to teach the Scriptures.

Paul documented his credentials in the third chapter of Philippians. He was "circumcised the eighth day" according to Jewish tradition. He was "of the stock of Israel" since his Jewish heritage traced back to Jacob and Rachel. He was "of the tribe of Benjamin,"

READ
COLOSSIANS 1:1

READ
COLOSSIANS 2:1

HIS BIRTH

the tribe that produced Israel's first king, Saul, for whom he may have been named. He was a "Hebrew of the Hebrews" since both his parents were Jews and he was raised as a strict Jew. He was "a Pharisee," a member of the legalistic Jewish sect and the son of a Pharisee. He was also "a persecutor of the church." Scripture says that he "made havoc of the church, entering every house, and dragging off men and women, committing them to prison" (Acts 8:3).

How does Paul describe himself in Colossians 1:1 and 1:23?

_____

_____

How does his preconversion identity compare with his postconversion identity? (*Compare Phil. 3:3–6 and Col. 1:1,23*)

_____

_____

_____

_____

_____

_____

_____

HIS REBIRTH

Acts 9:1–19 records the conversion and baptism of Saul of Tarsus. Read this passage; then briefly summarize the salvation testimony of Saul. _____

_____

_____

_____

_____

_____

Saul of Tarsus, who boasted of his persecution of the Christians, later experienced a dramatic conversion to faith in Jesus Christ. Paul was traveling to Damascus in approximately A.D. 34–35 to arrest Jewish people who had accepted Jesus as Messiah. Suddenly, Saul saw a bright light and heard God speak. Blind and helpless but obedient, he was led into Damascus to a disciple named Ananias, who told Saul he had been chosen as God's messenger to the Gentiles. By faith, Saul was saved, filled with the Holy Spirit, and called to ministry. He received his sight and was baptized.

After his conversion, Saul grew in his faith and began to preach Christ, first to his own people, the Jews, and then to the Gentiles. Though his parents had given him the name Saul, he became known by the name Paul, his official Roman name (Acts 13:9). As he traveled, Paul preached the gospel, started churches, and made disciples. His strong stand for Christ caused him to become the *persecuted*, not the *persecutor*.

Paul's life is characterized by many significant events including:

- First trip to Jerusalem in A.D. 37–38 (Acts 9:26–29)
- Second trip to Jerusalem in A.D. 48 (Acts 11:27–30)
- Philippi imprisonment in A.D. 58–60 (Acts 16:16–40)
- Caesarean imprisonment in A.D. 58–60 (Acts 23:23–26:32)
- Roman imprisonment in A.D. 60–63 (Acts 27–28)

Choose one of the above accounts in the life of Paul to read. After reading the passage carefully, write a short summary of the event.

_____

_____

_____

_____

_____

_____

During his ministry, the apostle Paul, along with other followers of Christ, embarked on mission trips to spread the gospel to unsaved people. Among his traveling companions were Barnabas, John Mark, Luke, Silas, and Timothy. The Holy Spirit blessed their endeavors as many people were saved and many churches were started. These four trips have become known as Paul's Missionary Journeys:

1. First missionary journey in A.D. 48–50 to Galatia and Cyprus (Acts 13–14)
2. Second missionary journey in A.D. 51–53 to Macedonia, Achaia, and Greece (Acts 15:39–18:22)
3. Third missionary journey in A.D. 54–57 to Asia and Greece (Acts 18:23–21:17)
4. Fourth missionary journey as he traveled to prison in Rome in A.D. 59–60 to Caesarea, Crete, Malta, and Rome (Acts 27–28)

If your Bible has a section of maps, find the Mediterranean Sea and trace the four missionary journeys of Paul the apostle. More than any other disciple, Paul touched the world of his day with the gospel.

HIS WRITINGS

Paul the apostle is certainly well known for his dramatic conversion, his faithful life, and his missionary journeys. But he is best known for his prolific biblical writing. This one man wrote thirteen books of the New Testament, letters to the Christians of his world. His epistles comprise one fifth of the entire Bible and contain many significant theological truths.

The book of Colossians was Paul's ninth letter, written in A.D. 60–63. Though there is some uncertainty about the precise dating of the Pauline Epistles, most modern theologians accept the following chronology:

1. 1 Thessalonians—A.D. 50–52
2. 2 Thessalonians—A.D. 51–52
3. Galatians—A.D. 55–57
4. 1 Corinthians—A.D. 56–57
5. 2 Corinthians—A.D. 56–57
6. Romans—A.D. 55–59
7. Ephesians—A.D. 60–63
8. Philippians—A.D. 60–63
9. Colossians—A.D. 60–63
10. Philemon—A.D. 60–63
11. 1 Timothy—A.D. 62–64
12. Titus A.D. 62–64
13. 2 Timothy—A.D. 66–67

Which of these letters written by Paul has strengthened you most spiritually? _____

Why? _____
_____
_____
_____
_____

HIS DEATH

According to Acts 28:30,31: "Paul dwelt two whole years in his own rented house, and received all who came to him, preaching the kingdom of God and teaching the things which concern the Lord Jesus Christ with all confidence, no one forbidding him."

Paul probably died in Rome during his imprisonment, though specific details about his death are uncertain. According to Christian tradition, Paul was beheaded outside of the city of Rome. Because he gave his life for the spreading of the gospel, Paul will always be one of the greatest martyrs of the faith.

Each of Paul's letters was written to a specific New Testament church congregation or individual, but all of his letters are also addressed to Christians today. While he did not always know his audience personally, he was aware of their circumstances and concerned about their challenges. This prison letter, written while Paul was imprisoned in Rome, was to be read aloud to a congregation as encouragement and warning. Let us examine the city, the church, and the conflict.

HIS AUDIENCE

Located in the southwest corner of Asia Minor, or present day Turkey, Colosse (pronounced koh-LAHS-sih) was a prominent city during the Greek period. However, by the time of Paul, this city had become overshadowed by many neighboring towns. Its greatest resource was its fertile land where sheep were raised for the wool industry. Colosse became famous for a certain dye for clothing which bears its name. Though its geographical location seemed ideal, Colosse and the Lycus River Valley experienced frequent earthquakes. In fact, the city was destroyed in A.D. 61 by a severe earthquake.

THE CITY

Search your New Testament map and locate the town of Colosse in southwest Asia Minor.

The church at Colosse consisted predominantly of Gentile believers with a small number of Jewish converts. Though Paul did not visit this area himself, the church was probably started during his evangelization of Ephesus. Epaphras (pronounced EP-uh-frass) is described as the faithful minister of the Colossian church (Col. 1:7; 4:12,13). He was also called "a fellow servant" of Paul.

THE CHURCH

Read these verses and describe the Christians in Colosse—Colossians 1:2,12,21,27._____

_____

_____

_____

_____

_____

THE CONFLICT

New Christians in the Colossian church were being challenged by false teaching or heresy. While numerous distorted viewpoints prevailed, the roots of gnostic thought were evident in Colosse at the time of Paul's letter. In general, gnosticism was the belief in a secret knowledge available to only a few people. Gnosticism has two basic assumptions: (1) the spirit alone is good and matter is evil, and (2) the universe is created out of matter which is both evil and eternal. Those teachings greatly affected the doctrine of creation, the gift of salvation, and the ethical approach to life. Thus a conflict arose between the Christians in Colosse and the false teachers.

Read Colossians 2:8–10 and write a warning to all Christians who encounter heresies. _____

_____

_____

_____

_____

_____

_____

HIS ADMONITION

Paul wrote his letters for the same reason people write letters and postcards today: to keep in touch with family and friends. Paul particularly wanted to stay in touch while traveling. This letter was written to his friends in Colosse. In fact, Paul desired for this letter to be read aloud to a congregation.

What impact does reading a letter aloud have on the listener?

_____

_____

_____

_____

Paul obviously wanted his message to be heard. He had a strong admonition for the Colossian Christians. His warning in Colossians 1:27,28 states his purpose: the gospel of Jesus Christ is for all people. Therefore, we are called by Christ to proclaim His truth to everyone—the Jews and Gentiles, people we know, and even strangers. That same message speaks to Christians today. We are to go into the whole world and share the good news of Jesus Christ with every man and woman.

In his short but powerful letter, Paul attempts to answer some difficult questions with practical theological insights. As a result, he develops several themes. These profound answers are practical guidelines for daily living. As you read the book of Colossians, notice these primary themes:

1. Christ is Creator of everything and Savior of all.
2. The world is sinful and seeking to devour all.
3. Christians are vehicles of service and examples of faith.

Grace to you and peace from God our Father and the Lord Jesus Christ" (Col. 1:2*b*).

Who are you? In many ways your identity is wrapped up in your relationship to Christ. Read these two passages of Scripture: Colossians 1:21–22 and Colossians 2:10.

How does Paul describe you? _____

_____

_____

_____

Now read 1 Peter 2:9–10.

List some words or phrases that identify who you are in Christ.

_____

_____

_____

_____

_____

Thank God for who you are and who He intends for you to be!

PRESCRIPTION 1 FOR SPIRITUAL WELLNESS

PERSONAL SPIRITUAL WELLNESS

COLOSSIANS 1:1–12

Most Christians receive great joy as they talk to the Father. But have you ever thought that prayer pleases God? The Lord wants to hear from His children. Though He already knows our thoughts and desires, God loves for us to voice our hearts to Him.

One prescription for spiritual wellness is prayer. Believers cannot grow in their faith without communicating with God. Prayer is an essential ingredient for spiritual growth. Jesus Himself commanded us to pray, but He didn't ask us to pray without teaching us how.

In the book of Colossians, we learn to pray by Paul's example and instruction. Initially Paul greeted the Christians in Colosse. Then he gave three specific ways to pray: lift up others, thank the Father, and ask for power. Carefully read Colossians 1:1–12 and underline any instructions about prayer.

LIFT UP OTHERS

Christians are greatly encouraged by the prayers of others. It is both a privilege and a responsibility to talk with God about the concerns of other people. Paul challenges us to lift up each other in prayer.

What specific prayer did Paul voice for the Colossians in verse 2?

He prayed: "_____ to you and _____ from God our Father and the Lord Jesus Christ."

Why is it important to pray for grace and peace for others?

_____

_____

_____

The most powerful prayer a Christian can pray for another Christian is for grace and peace. Grace is the unmerited gift of God which provides for our salvation. Peace is the sense of well-being regardless of outward circumstances. A believer needs grace for salvation and peace for Christian living.

Paul gave additional instruction in Colossians 1:1–12 on how to lift up others in prayer.

Read each of these verses from Colossians and write one guideline about praying for another person.

1:3 _____

1:9 _____

1:10 _____

1:11 _____

1:12 _____

While the Lord is eager to hear about our own needs, He is pleased when we talk with Him about others.

Look up the definition of the words *petition* and *intercession* in the dictionary. Compare these two forms of prayer. _____

_____
_____
_____
_____
_____
_____
_____
_____
_____
_____

While petition is the request a believer makes for her own needs, intercession is prayer focused on the needs of others. You may need to make a personal commitment to pray more faithfully for other people. Remember, God is pleased as you lift up others!

Jesus gave us a model for prayer in Matthew 6:5–15. His example teaches us to praise God for Who He is and what He has done, to ask Him for guidance, provision, and protection, and to seek forgiveness of sin. Though there are many helpful formats for prayer, prayer should provide opportunity for adoration, praise, thanksgiving, confession of sin, and requests for self and others.

Paul begins his prayer with "thanks to the God and Father of our Lord Jesus Christ" (Col. 1:3). He then lifts up others and prays for wisdom. He concludes this first section with more gratitude. What does Paul thank God for in Colossians 1:12?

One helpful format for prayer is represented by the acronym "ACTS." Certainly prayer should be an active process, with the believer speaking to the Father and listening to Him. As we pray, the four letters remind us of specific ways to pray.

A—Adoration
C—Confession
T—Thanksgiving
S—Supplication

Spend some time in prayer right now. Be sure to include in your prayer time some expression of adoration (praise for Who He is), confession (repentance of personal sin), thanksgiving (gratitude for what He has done), and supplication (requests for yourself and others).

Paul is quite clear in Colossians 1:9–12 about how to pray. He tells us to boldly and continuously ask for power as we pray for ourselves and for others. Specifically Paul says we are to:

- Ask for knowledge of God's will (1:9)
  —*then you will receive Scripture understanding.*
- Ask Him to help you walk worthy of the Lord (1:10)
  —*then you will please Him, be fruitful, and grow in knowledge of God.*
- Ask to be strengthened with all power (1:11)
  —*then you will attain patience and joy.*

Why do you think it is important for a Christian to pray for power?

_____

_____

_____

_____

How does God's power strengthen you each day?

_____

_____

_____

_____

_____

_____

Christians are to seek God's power, not for personal success, but in order to perform service for God. The believer is "strengthened with all power" in proportion to His power. If God is all-powerful (omnipotent), then the believer has unlimited power available for Christian living.

God's power is released through prayer! Paul had reason to praise the Lord in Colossians 1:12: "Giving thanks to the Father who has qualified us to be partakers of the inheritance of the saints in the light." God has qualified us to inherit His blessings. As a result, we should lift up others, thank the Father, and ask for prayer. As we do, we maintain spiritual wellness.

That you may have a walk worthy of the Lord, fully pleasing Him, being fruitful in every good work and increasing in the knowledge of God" (Col. 1:10).

How pleased is God with your prayer life? _____

_____

_____

_____

_____

Reflect on the time you have spent with the Lord this week, then write a prayer of recommitment to please God by faithful prayer.

_____

_____

_____

_____

_____

_____

_____

PRESCRIPTION 2 FOR SPIRITUAL WELLNESS

PERSONAL SPIRITUAL WELLNESS

$\mathcal{L}$ESSON THREE   THE INCOMPARABLE CHRIST

COLOSSIANS 1:13–23

Who is Christ? Earlier in our study you examined Colossians 1:21–22 to answer the question "Who are you?" Now let's examine this passage to better understand the nature of Jesus Christ. The first two chapters of Colossians are considered one of the great Christological passages. Christology is the study of Christ's nature and person. Other definitive Scriptures about Christ are: John 1 and 14; Philippians 2; and Hebrews 1 and 2.

An understanding of the person of Christ is essential to a believer's faith. The careful study of Scripture clarifies Who Christ is and sets the foundation for all other doctrines. Evangelical Christology accepts the two natures of Christ (God and man), without contradiction and without comparison. Colossians specifically addresses Christ as God Incarnate, Creator of the World, Head of the Church, and Reconciler of all.

CHRIST IS GOD INCARNATE

Before we begin an in-depth study of this passage, read Colossians 1:13–23.

List some of the qualities identified with Christ. You may want to note the specific Scripture reference._____

_____

_____

_____

_____

_____

_____

_____

_____

Colossians 1:15 clearly states that "Christ is the image of the invisible God, the firstborn over all creation."

What does Paul mean when he calls Christ the image of God?

_____

_____

_____

_____

_____

_____

The Greek word *eikon* which is translated "image" literally means "perfect manifestation." Jesus Christ is the perfect manifestation of God. He is 100 percent God. Christ is also God Incarnate. That means, He is God in the flesh, 100 percent man. Therefore, we accept the two natures of Christ. He is both God and man, divine and human, infinite and finite.

These facts about Jesus Christ are the essence of evangelical Christology:

1. Christ is 100 percent God and 100 percent man (John 1:1,14).
2. God was made flesh to live among us as Christ (Phil. 2:6–7).
3. Jesus was conceived by the Holy Spirit, born of the virgin Mary (Luke 1:35).
4. Though He lived in a sinful world, Jesus lived a perfect, sinless life (Matt. 5:48).
5. Christ died on the cross to pay the price of our sin (1 Peter 3:18).
6. His resurrection proved His deity and returned Him as a living presence with Christians (John 14:25–28).
7. Jesus reigns in heaven with God, eager to bring men to God (John 16:5–11).

Other beliefs about Jesus Christ are not biblical. Paul disputed the Colossian heresy by proclaiming Christ is God Himself.

The first verse of the Bible states clearly that God is the Creator of all that exists—"in the beginning God created the heavens and the earth" (Gen. 1:1).

What do these passages say about who created the world?

John 1:3 _____

Col. 1:16 _____

Heb. 1:2 _____

God alone created everything. He has always existed and spoke matter into existence. His words had the power of creation.

Read these verses in Genesis and briefly summarize the creative work of God.

Day 1 (Gen. 1:2–5)—He created _____
_____

Day 2 (Gen. 1:6–8)—He created _____
_____

Day 3 (Gen. 1:9–13)—He created _____
_____

Day 4 (Gen. 1:14–19)—He created _____
_____

Day 5 (Gen. 1:20–23)—He created _____
_____

Day 6 (Gen. 1:24–31)—He created _____
_____

Day 7 (Gen. 2:1–3)—He _____
_____

Paul made it very clear in Colossians 1:16 that God created everything. While the gnostics believed an inferior God was responsible for creation, Paul taught that God by His Son Jesus created all things. God created everything in heaven and earth, everything seen and unseen, all people and all powers. Everything was created by God, for His purpose, with His involvement.

CHRIST IS HEAD OF THE CHURCH

In Colossians, Paul described Christ as God, as Creator, and as "head of the body, the church" (1:18). The church is a group of believers meeting together to serve the Lord and spread the gospel. Several biblical pictures have been given to increase our understanding of the church's role. The church is described in Scripture as the people

15

of God (1 Pet. 2:9–10), a family of God (Gal. 6:10), the bride of Christ (2 Cor. 11:2), and the body of Christ (Col. 1:18).

The physical body needs various parts to help it function. In the same way, the church needs different members with different gifts to serve the Lord's purpose. The head is necessary to the body's life and direction. Christ is in control of the church, its faith, and its work.

Carefully study 1 Corinthians 12:12–27.

What did Paul say to the Christians in Corinth about the church?

_____

_____

_____

_____

_____

_____

Jesus Christ chose to be Head of the church so that He could be involved in our daily lives. Christ Who is God and Creator is also Head of the church. Paul also calls Jesus a "reconciler" (Col. 1:20). Reconciliation is a prominent theme among the writings of Paul. The Christians of the early church needed to hear the message of reconciliation. Christians today need to hear that same message.

Look in a dictionary for the meaning of the word reconciliation. Write a definition here._____

_____

_____

_____

_____

_____

Reconciliation is restoration of unity in a relationship where alienation has taken place. While the concept is found often in the New Testament, the term reconciliation is found only in Paul's epistles (Rom. 5:10–21; 2 Cor. 5:18–20; Eph. 2:16; Col. 1:20–21). Paul confronted disputes among believers, fighting among the heathen, and separation from God in his letters. God desires peace with His children and among all His children.

CHRIST IS RECONCILER OF ALL

16

Read Colossians 1:19–23 and in your Bible underline the words or phrases that answer these questions:

1. Who is the reconciler?
2. To whom are we reconciled?
3. What is the result of reconciliation?

Scripture teaches that we are reconciled by Christ through His death on the cross. In being reconciled to God, we can be reconciled to others. Restoration with God and others results in holy, blameless, godly living. Christ desires to be the Reconciler of all.

Your personal understanding of the nature of Christ is essential to your own faith and is also necessary for sharing the gospel. Stand firm on the truth of the Word that Jesus is "the Christ, the Son of the living God" (Matt. 16:16). As you stand firm in that belief, you will remain spiritually well.

PRESCRIPTION 3 FOR SPIRITUAL WELLNESS

He is the image of the invisible God, the firstborn over all creation" (Col. 1:15).

PERSONAL SPIRITUAL WELLNESS

Who is Christ? How does He reveal Himself to you each day? Write a list of specific ways that Christ makes Himself known to you on a daily basis. _____

_____

_____

_____

_____

_____

"A Hymn of Him"
(Col. 1:15-20)

(Section 1)   15a   Who is the image
                    of God, the invisible one
              15b   firstborn of all creation?
              Chorus: **He is the Christ, the Son of the
                        living God** (Matt. 16:16).

              16a   For in him everything was created
              16b   in the heavens and on the earth
              16c   the visible and the invisible
                        whether thrones or dominions
                        whether rulers or authorities.
              Chorus: **He is the Christ, the Son of the
                        living God** (Matt. 16:16).
              16d   Everything has been created
                    through him and unto him.

(Section 2)   17a   And he is before all things
              17b   and all things in him hold together.
              Chorus: **He is the Christ, the Son of the
                        living God** (Matt. 16:16).

(Section 3)   18a   And he is the head
                    of the body, the church.
              Chorus: **He is the Christ, the Son of the
                        living God** (Matt. 16:16).

(Section 4)   18b   Who is the beginning
              18c   the firstborn from the dead
              18d   so that in everything he might become pre-eminent.
              Chorus: **He is the Christ, the Son of the
                        living God** (Matt. 16:16).
                        For in him all God's fullness
                        was pleased to dwell
              Chorus: **He is the Christ, the Son of the
                        living God** (Matt. 16:16).
              20a   And through him to reconcile
                    everything to himself
              20b   making peace through the blood
                    of his cross (through him)
              20c   whether things on the earth
                    or things in the heavens.
              Chorus: **He is the Christ, the Son of the
                        living God** (Matt. 16:16).

Adapted from Wright, N. T. *Tyndale New Testament Commentaries: Colossians and Philemon* (Grand Rapids, Wm. B. Eerdmans Publishing Company, 1986).

COLOSSIANS 1:24–29

Paul attempted to give the Christians in Colosse, what we call in this study, a prescription for spiritual wellness.
First, he taught them by example and instruction how to pray. Then he clarified the nature and person of Christ. Next, Paul addressed the Christian life.

In Colossians 1:24–29, the apostle Paul considered three very specific challenges that Christians experience daily. He addressed these challenges of the Christian life: human suffering, the mysteries of our faith, and the call to service.

Suffering was known to Jesus and was not unusual to Paul or to Christians of the early church. Suffering is also a reality today. In many of his writings Paul encouraged believers to rejoice in affliction—physical, emotional, or spiritual. He tried to help them understand or accept the mysteries of their faith, and he reminded them of their role in spreading the gospel. Today, we still ask the same questions: Why do good people suffer? Why doesn't God make Himself known clearly to His children? Will what I am doing for God make a difference?

WE CAN REJOICE IN SUFFERING

Paul wrote about suffering from his prison cell in Rome (Acts 28:16,30). His attitude about suffering exemplifies the appropriate Christian response to hardship. Paul rejoiced in his suffering because he knew Christ had suffered greatly on his behalf and that his own suffering was for the glory of God. Christians today who are confident of their calling can rejoice in their suffering for the sake of the gospel.

**Scripture provides helpful insights for the suffering saints.
Read James 1:2–4 and answer this question: How should the**

Christian respond to suffering?_____
_____
_____
_____
_____

Because of our faith in God, Christians can face the inevitable trials with courage. Suffering, though painful, can result in spiritual maturity. In fact, there are blessings which can lead to joy as we suffer.

Paul suggested five reasons to rejoice in suffering. Can you experience these blessings even as you suffer?

1. Suffering brings believers closer to Christ (Phil. 3:10). While most Christians wouldn't choose to suffer, the pain of suffering often results in deeper fellowship with God.

2. Suffering assures the believer that she belongs to Christ (John 15:18–19). If Jesus suffered for His faith, other believers will too. The Holy Spirit's presence in our lives during suffering also assures our salvation.

3. Suffering brings a future reward (Rom. 8:18–25). The present sufferings on earth are insignificant in comparison to the glorious hope of eternal life.

4. Suffering is inevitable, but it is temporary (1 Peter 1:6). Though pain often seems to linger; for the believer, the time of suffering is fleeting since life is eternal.

5. Suffering for the sake of the gospel should be counted a privilege (2 Thess. 1:4-8). Though suffering is not pleasant, for the believer it is a high calling. God can use our suffering for His glory.

How have you handled suffering in your life?_____
_____
_____

What did God teach you during your trials?_____
_____
_____

God chose to reveal to Paul a mystery of the faith—the mystery that the gospel was for all people. That revelation was revolutionary for Paul, a Jew and a Pharisee. In addition, it was a mystery to Paul that God would call him to minister to the Gentiles. God chooses to reveal Himself and His mystery to the saints.

Who are the saints to whom God reveals His mystery?

_____

_____

_____

What are the results of that mystery? (*See Col. 1:26–27*)

_____

_____

_____

God does choose to reveal many truths to His children. However, there are some mysteries which remain unknown.

Read the following statements about the mystery of our faith, and determine if they are true or false. Circle T for true statements and F for false statements. You may need to check the Scripture reference for accuracy.

☐ T ☐ F   1. There are some things that God reveals to no one (Deut. 29:29).

☐ T ☐ F   2. Certain people learn some mysteries of God (Psalm 25:14).

☐ T ☐ F   3. The New Testament reveals some mysteries of the Old Testament (Col. 1:26).

☐ T ☐ F   4. The mysteries of God are revealed only to believers (1 Cor. 2:7–16).

☐ T ☐ F   5. Men do not discover the mysteries, God reveals them (Col. 1:27).

All of these statements are truths about the mysteries of the faith. Is there still mystery in your faith? Are there things about God you still

don't understand? In your own words, try to explain those mysteries. _____

_____

_____

_____

While we will not fully understand the Father until we are with Him in Heaven, He promises that we will understand the most important mystery—the mystery of the ages that Paul faced. Christ in you is the hope of glory (Col. 1:27). His message of hope and salvation is for all. That truth should motivate all believers to strive for the gospel. God chose to reveal that mystery to His children—to you!

Why should we work so hard for the gospel? Colossians 1:25 answers that question definitively. We are to work for the gospel because we are called to minister, we need to be good stewards of God's gifts, and we must fulfill the Word of God. A call to ministry is a very serious matter. God calls for a purpose—to accomplish His purpose here on earth.

Have you been called by God to work for Him? _____
Explain your call. _____

_____

_____

_____

_____

_____

WE CAN STRIVE FOR THE GOSPEL

Paul became a minister (Col. 1:23,25), a high calling from God to spread the gospel to all people. He was passionate about his call. In 1 Corinthians 9:16, Paul sincerely proclaimed, "For if I preach the gospel, I have nothing to boast of, for necessity is laid upon me; yes, woe is me if I do not preach the gospel!"

Pray for that same passion about God's calling in your life.

Christians are to be good stewards of their calling. We don't own the gospel. The gospel is the message of God. We have the responsibility of managing the gospel. Since He chose to reveal His mystery to us and since He has called us, we are obliged to share His gospel with others. Are you a good steward of the gospel?

When did you last share your faith with an unbeliever? _____

_____

_____

_____

_____

_____

As you record your response to that personal question, ask God to make you a faithful steward of the gospel.

Let's examine a final reason for Christians to strive for the gospel. The Bible challenges us to spread the gospel. Every believer chooses to obey or disobey God as we choose whether or not to strive for the gospel. In Colossians 1:28, Paul is specific in giving Christians instructions about how to spread the gospel.

Carefully read and reread that verse and make your gospel "to do" list below.

The Christian's To-Do List (*Col. 1:28*)

1. _____

2. _____

3. _____

Christians are to strive for the gospel daily. We must warn everyone, teach everyone, and present everyone perfect in Christ. That's a tall order! That's a big job! But Colossians tells us how to do it. Work hard and depend on God's power (Col. 1:29). Even the task of spreading the gospel to all people can be accomplished by the faithful labor of believers and the mighty power of God. As you toil for Him, rejoice! Rejoice in your suffering, rejoice in the mystery, and rejoice in your calling.

*T*o this end I also labor, striving according to his working which works in me mightily" (Col. 1:29).

In the paraphrase, *The Message*, Paul challenges Christians: "We preach Christ...that's what I'm working so hard at day after day, year after year, doing my best with the energy God so generously gives me" (Col. 1:28, 29).

What are you using your energy to proclaim? _____

_____

_____

_____

_____

_____

_____

BUILT UP IN CHRIST

COLOSSIANS 2:1–15

Bodybuilding is considered by many to be a sport. But is it really a sport? Men and women work hard to build and flex muscles, but what do they actually do with their strength? Some stand before judges and audiences in skimpy swimsuits posing their oiled bodies and their rippling muscles. They do not lift a weight, run a race, or win a game. They simply display their bodies.

Christ calls us to be built up in Him not just to look strong but to lift the weights of adversity, run the race with endurance, and win the game of life. In Colossians 2:6–7, Paul challenges Christians to be "rooted and built up in Him." The only reason for our spiritual strength is to serve the Lord and spread His gospel.

The Christian life should be more like a relay race; each believer, trained in the faith, should pass on the gospel with much haste to another person. Paul often wrote in his letters about running the race. Read Philippians 3:12–14 and record some of Paul's teachings about how Christians should run the race.

Are you running the race of faith? Are you passing the torch of the gospel? Are you winning the race of life?

Make a commitment to be rooted in Christ, built up in Him, and established in Him so that you can walk in Him each day.

ROOTED IN HIM

After his brief digression about suffering, Paul returned to his theme of Christ and the mystery of the gospel. He struggled as he walked with people in the faith and thought of the friends he had never met in the Lycus River Valley. Paul reflected on the Christians in the towns of Laodicea and Hierapolis, as well as Colosse, and hoped they would circulate his letter among their churches. He was passionate in his concern and practical in his counsel.

Believers are to be rooted in a person not a philosophy. Paul deeply desired for the Christians to place their faith in God and be rooted in His Word. Instead, many were believing the false teachings of gnosticism. To be rooted firmly in faith, believers must understand the mystery—there is one God for all and one way to salvation through Jesus Christ our Lord.

Read Colossians 2:1–7. How many verbs can you identify? What do these action words teach about growing a strong faith?

know (v. 1) _____

encourage (v. 2) _____

knit (v. 2) _____

say (v. 4) _____

receive (v. 6) _____

walk (v. 6) _____

If believers are to grow strong in the faith, we must walk daily in Christ—continuing to believe the truth about Him. Believers are to know the truth, encourage others in their faith, knit them together in love, say His truth persuasively, and receive Jesus Christ as Savior and Lord.

Just as a tree sinks its roots deeply in the rich soil, believers must root themselves deeply in Christ. Salvation begins the planting process and a relationship with Christ nourishes spiritual growth and produces fruit. Keep your life deeply rooted in Him!

BUILT UP IN HIM

For physical well-being, a woman must eat a balanced diet and exercise regularly. That daily regimen will build up or strengthen the body physically. Pamela Smith said, "Proper nutrition without exercise is like a car without tires—the body may look good, but it won't go anywhere!"[1] Spiritual well-being is the same. A believer must learn faith in Christ and abound in it in order to be spiritually strong (see Col. 2:7).

When a person wants to lose weight, she is tempted to take short cuts by trying a crash diet or taking diet pills. Though she may lose weight quickly, she rarely sustains the weight loss. Medical experts recommend a combination of proper nutrition and exercise to gradually reduce weight. Another result is a healthier lifestyle. Some believers are also tempted to accept false teachings and believe deceptive doctrine. Read Colossians 2:8–10. Paul strongly warned believers not to settle for less than the truth.

Write Paul's warning in Colossians 2:8 in your own words.

_____

_____

_____

_____

_____

_____

Only in Christ does the fullness of God dwell (Col. 2:9–10). In the musical *God With Us*, the narrator recites the names of God given in the Bible from Genesis to Revelation. It is thrilling to hear the 66 names of God, from "The Ram at Abraham's Altar" in Genesis to "The King of Kings and Lord of Lords" in Revelation. In the book of Colossians, God is called "fullness of the Godhead bodily" (Col. 2:9). Knowing Who God is and how He works in lives is essential to faith. Only through a knowledge of God and a steadfast walk in faith is a believer complete (Col. 2:10). God the Creator, Who revealed Himself to us in His Son Jesus Christ and the Holy Spirit, dwells in every believer and builds us up.

Without God, a person is incomplete. Without God, there is an emptiness. Without God, there is a piece missing, a lack of strength. The philosopher and scientist Blaise Pascal said, "There is a God-shaped vacuum in every heart." St. Augustine prayed, "Our hearts are restless until they find rest in thee." Recently my husband, Dr. Chuck Kelley said, "Jesus is the missing piece to the puzzle of our soul." Each statement clearly challenges all people to fill their emptiness with Jesus, to find rest in Him, and to be complete in Him. Ephesians 6:10 says, "Be strong in the Lord and in the power of His might." Therefore, put your faith in Him and let Him build you up.

ESTABLISHED IN HIM

To be strong in the Lord, believers must be rooted in Him, built up in Him, and established in Him. Paul gave specific instructions in Colossians 2:7, "Be established in the faith." What does it mean to be established? The dictionary defines the verb *establish* in several ways: "to make stable, make firm, settle; to order, ordain or enact permanently." One of those definitions relates directly to Paul's instruc-tion in Colossians 2:11–15. Carefully read this passage. Paul exhorted believers to establish their faith through the ordinance of baptism.

An ordinance is a symbolic act set into practice by Jesus Christ. In Colossians 2:11, Paul first explained about salvation. We learn that salvation is not just for the Jew who was physically circumcised. Salvation by faith in Jesus Christ is for all and results in a spiritual circumcision—freedom from the power of the flesh. Then Paul described New Testament baptism. Baptism is for believers and symbolizes the death and resurrection of Jesus, while also depicting the death of "the old person" and the resurrection of "a new person" (Col. 2:12). Though baptism is not necessary for salvation, it is an act of obedi-ence which demonstrates our faith.

Baptism is important for believers. It affirms faith personally and expresses the gospel publicly. A believer's baptism should be celebrated.

Can you think of ways to make the ordinance of baptism special to a new convert? List a few suggestions here. _____

_____

_____

_____

_____

_____

_____

_____

The point is this: baptism is to be a public display of the personal faith of a believer. It can be an effective way to explain the gospel to the lost.

Paul concluded this section in the second chapter of Colossians with a description of forgiveness. The forgiveness of Jesus Christ is different from human forgiveness.

What do these phrases in Colossians 2 teach about forgiveness of sin?

• **"forgiven you all trespasses" (v. 13):**_____

_____

_____

- "wiped out what was against us" (v. 14): _____

_____

_____

- "taken it out of the way" (v. 14): _____

_____

_____

While our debt of sin resulted from violation of the law of God (sin), Jesus Christ completely paid the price for our sin. He canceled our debt. Only when a believer understands the mystery of salvation does she have the whole picture.

In Colossians 2:2–3, Paul provided a beautiful biblical picture which can speak to women today. He encouraged believers to be "knit together with love." A knitted garment is such a gift of love. Knitters invest many hours to create a beautiful pattern from strings of yarn. Love is woven into each stitch.

However, we do not fully appreciate the special work of art until the project is complete. Then, we understand completely, and the uncertainty is revealed. As believers, our pieces of life are knitted together with love. But the total picture is not complete unless the believer is rooted in Him, built up in Him, and established in Him.

PRESCRIPTION 5 FOR SPIRITUAL WELLNESS

"As you have therefore received Christ Jesus the Lord, so walk in Him" (Col. 2:6).

PERSONAL SPIRITUAL WELLNESS

How strongly are you built up in Christ?
Examine your spiritual strength in the same way a doctor might examine your physical strength. How many pounds are you lifting daily in your spiritual life? Use a scale of 1 to 10, with 10 being the heaviest weight. Be honest in your estimation.

Bible study _____ lbs.

Prayer _____ lbs.

Witnessing _____ lbs.

Service _____ lbs.

Are you a weakling or a superwoman? _____

What is your new spiritual fitness program?_____

_____

_____

_____

_____

_____

[1]Pamela M. Smith, *Food for Life* (Lake Mary, Fla.: Creation House, 1994), 136.

COLOSSIANS 2:16–23

Have you ever experienced the diet principle? Simply stated it is the physical and psychological phenomenon of increased hunger when a diet is begun. Isn't that true? If you decide to lose weight, you immediately desire to eat more food. Negative reinforcement seems to increase the appetite. While hard to explain, its reality is evident. The more you try not to eat, the more you want to eat.

In Paul's time the roots of gnosticism and Jewish legalism were prevalent. False teaching not only limited knowledge to the spiritual elite; it added works to salvation by faith. Regulations and practices developed to measure spirituality and add to the Christian belief that Christ alone is sufficient for salvation.

Christ came to fulfill the law and to provide salvation through faith alone. Therefore, our faith is not dependent on adherence to rules and regulations, but on personal belief in Jesus Christ as Savior. For the Christian, all her cravings can be met in Christ. Salvation by faith should satisfy the believer's appetite. Are you spiritually satisfied?

THE ADDITIVES TO FAITH

Jewish legalists and those involved in gnostic thought added works to faith. They insisted on behavioral practices to ensure salva-tion. Spiritual additives, like their laws and observances, are just as unhealthy as physical additives. The additives in food not only take away from the natural flavor, but they add substances which are un-natural and often harmful to the body. Spiritual additives in turn take away from the pure truth and add unnecessary human effort.

Carefully read Colossians 2:16–23. These verses refer to four specific practices of some people in Colosse. After you read the

description of each false teaching, record a Scripture verse or verses in this passage which address that particular teaching.

1. Asceticism—Some believed that all matter is essentially evil, and they went to extremes to limit what a person ate or drank. Extensive regulations were developed to list clean and unclean foods. They practiced legalistic obedience to the letter of the law.

What verses in Colossians 2:16–23 address this practice? _____

_____

2. Observation of days—In addition to food regulations, some of the Colossians identified lists of days which belonged to God. They observed yearly feasts, monthly new moons, and weekly Sabbaths with elaborate ritual. The focus was on adherence to the ritual not worship of God.

What verse in this passage warns about this practice? _____

_____

3. Special visions—Some people believed that divine knowledge was limited to only the elite intellectuals. Therefore, it was common for certain individuals to boast about special revelations and interpretive power. These mystics spoke of visions which they felt the ordinary man couldn't see or understand. They prided themselves in a false godliness. Paul warned the Christians in Colosse about these false teachers.

What verse in this passage records his warning about this practice?

_____

4. Worship of angels—With their strong belief in angels and the work of many spiritual intermediaries, many people began to worship angels in the same way they worshiped God. Paul reminded the Colossian Christians that worship was reserved for God and Jesus Christ alone. While angels do minister to believers, they are only messengers of God. They are not God and are not worthy of worship (Heb. 1:14).

What verses specifically discuss this practice? _____

_____

THE DIET GURU

Throughout history, people have resorted to elevating humans to a pedestal rather than clinging to God alone as divine. It is easier for some to trust the words of an apparently inspired person who can be seen and touched than to have faith in an invisible though ever-present God and His inspired Word, the Bible. The gnostics followed false prophets who thought they were the only ones to receive wisdom from God. Paul reminded the Christians that God speaks directly to His children. He warned them about letting spiritual leaders dictate behavior and cast judgment (Col. 2:16–18).

Richard Simmons is a modern day diet guru. His energetic exercise videos and highly regulated diet plan have helped many people lose weight. However, many of his followers credit him personally for their weight loss and not the exercise program or proper nutrition. Often people find it easier to follow people than to follow God.

There is also a risk in following spiritual gurus. Some cults today exercise more faith in an individual than faith in God. The leader's personal experience may be assigned universal meaning. Therefore, followers blindly obey the guru and become a literal clone. This is an extreme example of the guru principle. However, many Christians today who love a pastor or Bible study teacher may listen more obediently to that person than they do to the Word of God. Paul challenges Christians to "hold fast to the Head" (Col. 2:19). The Head of the Church is Jesus Christ.

While Christians must avoid following human gurus, the importance of Christian examples cannot be overlooked. In her book, *A Garden Path to Mentoring*, Esther Burroughs defines mentoring as "pouring your love for God into another."[1] Numerous Scriptures teach the importance of mentoring (for example, Titus 2:1–5). To be a godly mentor you must first understand the meaning of mentor.

Contrast the difference between a guru and a mentor. _____
_____
_____
_____
_____
_____
_____
_____
_____
_____
_____
_____

In a personal tribute, Melody Burroughs Reid said about her mother, "She is my best friend, my hero, and my mentor, always pointing me in the direction of Jesus Christ."[2] The key difference is that while a human guru draws attention to self, a spiritual mentor points a person to Jesus.

An important lesson can be learned from the guru principle. While others can be an example of godly living, Christ alone is our model of righteousness. Beware of following others rather than imitating Christ! As a believer, you are responsible for your own spirituality. While other Christians may serve as mentors to you, no one can relate to God for you.

In this final section of Colossians 2, Paul warned the Colossians about adding regulations to their faith and about following spiritual gurus. Those who followed these practices were spiritually unhealthy. They were not a part of the work of Christ, and they were not growing in their faith. They were guilty of several false teachings. First, they understood only half truths (Col. 2:16–23). Their faith was dependent only on observance of regulations, not personal relationship with Christ. Second, they practiced false humility (Col. 2:18,23). They believed few people were worthy of access to God. Christianity professes a salvation for all. Third, they exhibited sinful pride (Col. 2:18,23). They boasted of spiritual knowledge and intellectual elitism. And fourth, they supported unnecessary slavery to ritual and routine (Col. 2:20,23). The adherence to strict rules and regulations imposes bondage and negates freedom in Christ. Christ's death on the cross provided liberty for all believers, freedom from the power and penalty of sin.

What regulations and rules are you following that rob you of your freedom in Christ? _____

_____

_____

_____

_____

_____

_____

_____

_____

_____

Paul taught release from the legalism of regulations and participation in the work of the church. For the Christian, there is freedom in Christ. Since Christ alone provides for our salvation by faith in Him, we do not have to live by a set of rules or regulations. The lives of believers are not built on a list of "do nots." Those human guidelines are of no value against fleshly indulgence (Col. 2:23). Instead, God provided salvation through His Son Jesus Christ, Who paid the price for our sins. Salvation is an act of God, not the action of people. While a believer's behavior does not produce salvation, godly behavior is an evidence of salvation.

PRESCRIPTION 6
FOR SPIRITUAL
WELLNESS

*T*herefore, if you died with Christ from the basic principles of the world, why, as though living in the world, do you subject yourselves to regulations" (Col. 2:20).

PERSONAL
SPIRITUAL
WELLNESS

Carefully read Colossians 2:20. Then read Paul's similar statement of faith in Galatians 2:18–21. Now write the meaning of Colossians 2:20 in your own words. _____

_____

_____

_____

_____

_____

_____

_____

_____

_____

_____

_____

_____

[1]Burroughs, Esther, *A Garden Path to Mentoring: Planting Your Life in Another and Releasing the Fragrance of Christ* (Birmingham: New Hope, 1997), 7.

[2] *Ibid.*, back cover.

COLOSSIANS 3:1–11

A wide discrepancy developed between legalistic Jewish ritual and undisciplined behavior which God freely forgives. On the one hand, false teachers taught strict adherence to the letter of the law while new Christians believed in Christ's forgiveness of all sin. A chasm developed separating the works-based view of salvation (Col. 2:20) from the Christians' understanding of salva-tion by faith (Col. 3:2). Dangers are inherent in both. Some in Colosse began to worry about salvation based on their effort alone. The Christians expressed little concern about their behavior since sins are forgiven by God. The Scripture warns about both perspectives.

Paul confronted those adhering to works-based salvation of the gnostics in Colossians 2 when he said, "If you died with Christ from the basic principles of the world, why, as though living in the world, do you subject yourselves to regulations" (verse 20). However, he quickly warned believers in chapter 3 about carnal behavior (see verses 1–11). While salvation comes by faith alone, godly living is a natural result of salvation. The focus of Colossians is on a personal relation-ship with God, not a perfect practice of the law.

Most Christians would worry themselves to death if their own actions determined their salvation. Worry is not conducive to good physical health and it undermines spiritual health as well. In another letter, Paul discussed anxiety. "Be anxious for nothing, but in every-thing by prayer and supplication, let your requests be made known to God" (Phil. 4:6). He warned Christians not to worry, because worrying doesn't help. God's work, not our worry, makes a difference!

Jesus Christ pleaded with His disciples not to worry. Three times in Matthew 6:25–34, He said, "Do not worry." He assured them and He assures us that He will provide for all our needs, even our greatest need—salvation. Worry takes the focus off of Christ and His ample provision for all of our needs. In truth, worry waters down our faith. Our faith is dependent on God's love for us, not our own actions. While our actions don't determine our salvation, our behavior is important to God. He promises to forgive sin, but He rejoices when He observes godly living. Read Colossians 3:1–11 to understand Christ's desire for our healthy Christian living. As Paul begins, he reiterates a strong conviction, "If then you were raised with Christ, seek those things which are above, where Christ is, sitting at the right hand of God" (Col. 3:1). If you are saved and desire to live for Christ, you will be consistent, real, and godly.

So if you're serious about living this new resurrection life with Christ, act like it" (Col. 3:1, *The Message*). Paul is very direct when he confronts the Colossian Christians. If you are a Christian, act like it! The greatest challenge facing Christians today is living out our faith. It is essential for the Christian's lifestyle to be consistent with the Christian faith. Living a consistent life of Christlikeness day after day is also important.

In the late 1800s, a godly Christian woman named Hannah Whitall Smith became concerned about the inconsistencies in the lives of professed Christians. She expressed her concern in the book, *The Christian's Secret to a Happy Life*. This same concern could be voiced today. "The standard of practical holy living has been so low among Christians that very often the person who tries to practice spiritual disciplines in everyday life is looked upon with disapproval by a large portion of the Church. And for the most part, the followers of Jesus Christ are satisfied with a life so conformed to the world, and so like it in almost every respect, that to a casual observer, there is no difference between the Christian and the pagan."[1]

Several years ago, my husband was leading an evangelism training conference in Las Vegas, Nevada. As he waited at the airport to depart the "gambling capital of the world," he was tempted to try out a slot machine. He was simply curious and initially thought it would be okay to gamble just once. But then the Lord convicted him to live out his faith—to practice what he preached. So he didn't put the quarter in the machine. As he boarded the plane, a man from the church said, "Hi Preacher. I've been watching you to see if you would gamble when you thought nobody was looking." His testimony would have been tarnished if his life hadn't been consistent with his faith.

How can you be consistent in your Christian living? In Colossians 3:2, Paul says, "Set your mind on things above, not on things on the earth." What does this verse teach you about how to be consistent in your Christian living?

The Lord truly desires for us to be consistent in living out our faith. "Walk the talk" is a key prescription to healthy Christian living. Live out your faith.

BE REAL

It is important to the Christian's witness for her lifestyle to be consistent with her faith. It is also essential for the Christian to be real—genuine, honest, truthful. When God changes a person's heart, He creates a new person. The old person dies and the "real person" is created in the image of God. In Colossians 3:5, Paul advises Christians to "put to death your members which are on earth." Christians are not to literally kill themselves, but to continually extinguish evil desires or lusts.

In the following two verses, Paul interrupted the list of sins to explain why changing from our sinful ways and becoming a new creation is so essential. First, we are reminded that sin brings God's judgment. Colossians 3:6 says, "Because of these things, the wrath of God is coming." Wrath is God's intentional reaction to sin.

What do these verses teach about the wrath of God?

John 3:36 _____

_____

Romans 1:18 _____

_____

Romans 2:5 _____

_____

1 Thessalonians 1:10 _____

_____

What do you know personally about the wrath of God?

_____
_____
_____
_____
_____
_____

A second reason for believers to put sin to death (Col. 3:5) is that sin is a part of the believer's past. After conversion, sinfulness is no longer acceptable. It becomes deception when an individual professes faith and lives a sinful life. That ungodly lifestyle was a part of the old self, the life without Christ (Col. 3:7). To continue in sin after salvation is to live a lie, to be deceptive to the world.

Being a fake, pretending, or keeping up a facade is difficult. My husband and I visited a college friend several years after graduation. As she discussed her involvement in church (singing in the choir, teaching Sunday School), we were thrilled with her apparent strong faith. Only later did we learn that she was having an affair with a married man. She had not given us the full picture. In fact, she had been deceptive and dishonest. She had not died to her sinful ways. Don't live a lie! Be real. Act out your faith and live a healthy Christian life.

BE GODLY

In the final verses of Colossians 3:1–11, Paul contrasts the "old man" and the "new man." He clearly exhorts believers to put off the sinful ways of the old man and put on the godly ways of the new man.

Carefully read verses 8 through 14. List below the behaviors to be "put off" and those to be "put on" by the believer.

Put Off (*Col. 3:8–9*) _____

_____

Put On (*Col. 3:12–14*) _____

_____

Paul also contrasted the life of the old man and the new man in Galatians 5. In verses 19 through 21, he tells Christians to avoid deeds of the flesh such as adultery, idolatry, jealousy, and heresy. In verses 22 and 23, he calls believers to a new life evidenced by the fruit of the Holy Spirit (love, joy, peace, patience, kindness, goodness, faithfulness, gentleness, and self-control). A healthy Christian is a holy Christian—a believer living a godly life. If your desire is to maintain spiritual wellness, your faith must be consistent, real, and godly.

In reflecting back on Colossians 3:1–11, there are several helpful hints for healthy Christian living.

Refer to the specific Scriptures and fill in the blanks to complete each statement.

1. Seek _____ (3:1).

2. Set your mind on _____ (3:2).

3. Put to death _____ (3:5).

4. Be renewed in _____ (3:10).

This passage gives us a powerful prescription for spiritual wellness.

PRESCRIPTION 7
FOR SPIRITUAL
WELLNESS

$\mathcal{S}$et your mind on things above, not on things on the earth" (Col. 3:2).

PERSONAL
SPIRITUAL
WELLNESS

Is your daily life an accurate reflection of your faith? Are you consistent in your walk and your talk? Write a sentence to describe your faith in God. _____

_____

_____

Now write a sentence to describe your life today. _____

_____

_____

Are you consistent in your Christian living? _____

[1]Smith, Hannah Whitall, The Christian's Secret to a Happy Life (Westwood, NJ: Barbour and Company, Inc., 1985), 205

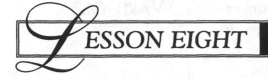

LESSON EIGHT — DRESS FOR SUCCESS

COLOSSIANS 3:12–17

While God is most concerned about inner beauty, women are often more interested in outer beauty. We spend hours each day trying to improve our appearance. Many of us carefully shop for just the right clothing. Our wardrobe in many ways is a reflection of who we are.

What if you were going on a trip and could only pack eight items of clothing. What eight pieces of clothing would you choose to take?

1. _____

2. _____

3. _____

4. _____

5. _____

6. _____

7. _____

8. _____

Women today do struggle when selecting a wardrobe. When we did this activity in our ladies Bible study, there were so many questions before answers could be given. Where were we going? How long would we be gone? Does underwear count as a piece of clothing? Such serious considerations about clothing. God desires for us to be just as conscientious about our spiritual wardrobe as we are about our personal one.

What is hanging in your closet right now? I am trying to find the time to clean out my closet. There are clothes that no longer fit or are no longer in style. Some clothes need mending and some outfits need updating. I strive to have in my closet all the basic clothing items I need to be properly dressed for every season and every occasion, because I always want to look my best.

A recent ladies clothing catalog included helpful suggestions about how to dress for success. They listed an eight-piece wardrobe that would guarantee that a woman would have something appropriate to wear for every occasion. I quickly went to my closet for an inventory and found my wardrobe lacking in several areas. Do you have these eight basic items of clothing in your closet?

1. A basic jacket
2. A tailored dress
3. Some twill pants
4. A classic shirt
5. A flattering skirt
6. A colorful scarf
7. Some comfortable shoes
8. A sturdy purse

If we spend so much time worrying about our personal wardrobe, shouldn't we spend even more time preparing our spiritual wardrobe? In Colossians 3:12–17, Paul gives some helpful hints about our spiritual wardrobe. As Christian women, we must look our best for Him at every occasion. Prayerfully read this passage, giving special attention to those virtues we must wear in order to bring glory to God. Paul suggests an eight-piece spiritual wardrobe.

1. *Put on tender mercies.* In the Old Testament, the Hebrew word *chesed* is translated "mercy" and literally means "unfailing love." God Himself is merciful, and He desires for His children to care for others. Mercy is a spiritual gift given by God so that believers will feel genuine empathy and compassion for others.

Read Acts 9:36–42. How did Dorcas wear tender mercy?_____

2. *Put on kindness.* Kindness has been defined as "steadfast love expressed in actions." God is kind to His children and to all people (Psalm 31:21). He commands His children to be kind to other believers and to other people (Eph. 4:32). Kindness is a fruit of the Holy Spirit, a virtue to be added to faith.

Read 2 Corinthians 6:3–10. Why must believers wear kindness?

_____

_____

_____

3. Put on humility. By nature we are often proud or boastful. The Bible says that "love is not puffed up" (1 Cor. 13:4). Humility is dependence on God and respect for others. Believers are to put God and others before self. Humility gives praise to the power of God not the works of man.

Read Matthew 5:3. What is received by believers who wear humility? _____

_____

4. Put on meekness. Weakness and meekness are not the same. Meekness is a positive quality of gentleness and sensitivity. Submission to God and personal self-control are reflected through sweet spirit and pleasant countenance. Meekness has been described as strength under control.

Read Matthew 5:5. What is the reward of those who are meek?

_____

5. Put on longsuffering. Patience is an attribute of God (Psalm 86:15), a fruit of the Holy Spirit in the believer's life (Gal. 5:22), and an attitude of the heart (1 Cor. 13:4). It is a difficult virtue to develop. The Greek word translated "patience" literally means "bear up under." Believers need to have patience with God, with self, and with others.

Read James 1:2–4. What can be used to produce patience? _____

_____

6. Put on tolerance. Some people and some things are easy to tolerate or put up with, others are not. The Lord endures all things for all times. He calls on His children to wait on Him and to tolerate each other.

Read Proverbs 25:15. What kind of tolerance is often needed to persuade a ruler? _____

_____

7. Put on forgiveness. God's forgiveness is complete, everlasting, and always available. Because God forgives, believers can forgive. Forgiveness is provided by God through an act of obedience. Forgiveness is a personal work by the Holy Spirit and a powerful witness to others.

Read Matthew 6:15. Why is it important for believers to forgive?

_____

_____

8. Put on love. Loving everybody is not easy. True love is unselfish, loyal, and benevolent concern for others. It is a fruit of the Holy Spirit, the greatest gift of all (1 Cor. 13:13). Christian love is eternal; it never fails. The Greek word *agape* is an action word meaning "Christlike, selfless love." Above all, the Lord wants us to put on love.

Read 2 John 5–6. What happens when believers wear love?

_____

_____

A PROTECTIVE WARDROBE

In Colossians 3:12–17, Paul speaks of a spiritual wardrobe. He lists the Christian virtues we are to put on. But in another New Testament letter, Paul teaches about a wardrobe for warfare.

Read Ephesians 6:13–18 and in your Bible underline your battle gear.

Dressing protectively for spiritual warfare is important for Christians. Every believer inherits the blessings of God but also the attack of God's enemies. As Satan bombards the believer with temptation, destruction, discouragement, and distraction, Christians must depend on the power of the Holy Spirit for protection. Only then can we withstand evil. In the same way a mother would provide a heavy coat for a child to survive cold temperatures, the Lord provides a protective wardrobe for His children to resist the evil one.

Refer back to Ephesians 6:13–18 and describe God's protective wardrobe against spiritual warfare.

> Ephesians 6:14—belt of _____
> Ephesians 6:14—breastplate of _____
> Ephesians 6:15—shoes of the _____
> Ephesians 6:16—shield of _____
> Ephesians 6:17—helmet of _____
> Ephesians 6:17—sword of _____

How do we obtain this armor of God? The answer is in Ephesians 6:18: " Pray always." Prayer is the key to resisting spiritual warfare. Prayer releases God's power to work in our lives, even to defeat the devil. Constant communication with God gives the believer direction and provision. Supplication for others protects them from evil and strengthens the believer who prays from the heart.

What a stunning spiritual wardrobe! If you put on these virtues, you will always be dressed for success. If you wear the armor of God, you will always be protected from spiritual warfare. Now may be the time to inventory your closet, to do some mending, or to give some old clothes away. Let the Lord dress you for His glory!

PRESCRIPTION 8 FOR SPIRITUAL WELLNESS

*B*ut above all these things put on love, which is the bond of perfection" (Col. 3:14).

PERSONAL SPIRITUAL WELLNESS

Take an inventory of your spiritual wardrobe. First, decide what ungodly behaviors you need to "take off" (anger, covetousness, lying, etc.). List them here. _____
_____
_____

Now determine what Christian virtues you need to "put on" (mercy, kindness, humility, etc.). List below the virtues to add to your spiritual wardrobe. _____
_____
_____

LESSON NINE — A SUBMISSIVE HEART

COLOSSIANS 3:18 – 4:1

Who has authority in your life? In your family, in your work, in your church, and among your friends, there are individuals who have been assigned leadership responsibility in our lives. As a young bride, I struggled with personal submission until I understood God's design for order in relationships. You may have struggled with this issue as well. In fact, it is natural for humans to resist the control of others.

For generations, submission has been a perplexing topic of discussion for Christians. Women have struggled to balance the tension between the biblical mandate to submit and the personal desire for independence. Society would have Christian women believe that submission is surrendering self and succumbing to the total control of another. In fact, the human distortion of this biblical teaching at times results in abuse and tyranny. God did not intend for His children to "lord over" each other. Instead He instituted submission to give order and clear authority to the relationships in life. Authority does not mean superiority.

The Greek word *hupotass* translated "submissive" literally means "to place under" or "to line up under." In His divine wisdom, God knew that authority must be established for human relationships to function effectively. So He gave clear instructions about how to relate to each other. God desires first for His children to willingly submit to Him—to give Him total control of life. Then He commands us to be submissive to others.

Read the following Scriptures which teach about biblical submission. Think carefully about how each teaching affects your life.

1. Hebrews 12:9—Submit first to God.
2. Romans 13:1–2—All authority is ordained by God.

3. 1 Peter 3:1–2—Choose to submit. Submission is an act of the will.
4. Eph. 5:21–24—Submission pleases God.
5. Eph. 5:25—Submission is a response to love.

Now write your own definition of biblical submission._____

_____

_____

_____

_____

_____

The Bible teaches all believers to totally surrender to the Lord and mutually submit to one another. Carefully read Colossians 3:18–4:1, then fill in the blanks below.

Wives submit to _____ (v. 18).

Husbands love _____ (v. 19).

Children obey _____ (v. 20).

Fathers do not provoke _____ (v. 21).

Servants obey _____ (v. 22).

Masters be fair to _____ (v. 4:1).

Now let's examine God's plan for these human relationships.

Throughout Scripture God uses the marriage relationship to teach important truths. He taught about His role in the church by using a marital analogy. The church is called the "bride of Christ" (2 Cor. 11:2). Therefore, Christ is understood to be the bridegroom of the church, the head of the body of Christ, the one in authority over all believers.

Scripture assigns a specific role to the husband and the wife in marriage. Different roles do not affect the worth of an individual. God created male and female in His own image, equal in worth and value, but different in role and function (Gen. 1:27). These roles help maintain order and establish authority in marriage. The Bible teaches that submission is an important part of marriage.

WIVES AND HUSBANDS

Reread these three passages to better understand biblical submission.

Ephesians 5:21–22
Colossians 3:18
1 Peter 3:1

While voluntary surrendering of self is difficult, it is God's plan. Understanding submission is a great challenge, but an even greater challenge is for a couple to demonstrate a submissive spirit every day.

Consider the following ways wives are to submit to their husbands. The Amplified translation of Ephesians 5:33 says, "Let the wife see that she respects and reverences her husband, that she notices him, honors him, prefers him, venerates and esteems him, and that she defers to him, praises him, regards him, and loves and admires him exceedingly." This Scripture paraphrase cites eight specific ways to show submission to your husband.

1. *Notice him.* Wives should pay attention to their husbands and not ignore them.

2. *Honor him.* Wives should respect their husbands, not put them down or belittle them.

3. *Prefer him.* Wives should desire to be with their husbands, enjoying them and enjoying spending time together.

4. *Venerate and esteem him.* Wives should appreciate and cherish their husbands. Consider husbands worthy and valuable.

5. *Defer to him.* Wives should support the decisions of their husbands.

6. *Praise him.* Wives should affirm and encourage their husbands. Affirmation is a basic need of most men.

7. *Regard him.* Women should affirm their husbands and the efforts their husbands make to lead the family.

8. *Love him.* Wives should care deeply for their husbands, expressing affection and care.

9. *Admire him exceedingly.* Wives should be devoted to their husbands, acknowledging their strengths.

While submission seems to be an overwhelming responsibility for the wife, husbands are to love their wives as much as Christ loves the church (Eph. 5:25–27). Paul used five verbs to describe Christ's relationship to His bride—the church. He loved her, gave Himself for her, sanctified her, cleansed her, and presented her to Himself. Christ expressed sacrificial love to His bride so that she could be complete. Husbands are to love their wives sacrificially and strengthen each other through the unity of marriage.

In Colossians 3:19, Paul warns husbands not to be bitter. This warning about bitterness is not recorded in any other Scripture referring to the role of husbands. Why do you think Paul voiced this concern at this time? Biblical love is expressed in both words and actions. Husbands must be careful to state their love and live it out. A wife often measures a husband's love by the way he treats her. If she does not consistently experience love, she can develop bitterness. In addition, a husband can become bitter toward his wife if he is resentful about his responsibilities or disappointed in her. Paul reminds husbands to love their wives and not treat them harshly.

CHILDREN AND PARENTS

Jesus modeled biblical submission for us. He submitted Himself completely to God (Luke 22:41–3). He was submissive to governmental authorities (Luke 22:47–54) and He was submissive to others (John 13:1–7). Jesus Christ was also submissive to His earthly parents, Joseph and Mary (Luke 2:46–52). The Bible does assign parents and children a reciprocal responsibility. While children are to obey their parents, parents are not to provoke or exasperate their children.

All children are to obey their parents. The Greek word for children (*tekna*) is a general term for children, not limited to a specific age group. The Greek word for obey (*hupakouete*) means continually obeying. In other words, children should continue always to obey their parents. Why? Paul stated the motive for obedience. It is "well pleasing to the Lord" (Col. 3:20).

In Ephesians 6:4 and Colossians 3:21, fathers are addressed directly. Previously both parents are mentioned, but now Paul focuses on the father. Typically the mother is the nurturer in the home and the father is the disciplinarian. Paul warns fathers not to provoke or irritate their children, as they might become discouraged or disheartened. Instead fathers are to train their children in the Lord.

Can you think of some ways that fathers can exasperate their children? List them here. _____

_____

_____

Children could be easily exasperated by the harshness or strictness of a father. However, they can be encouraged and strengthened by their fathers' love. Fathers need to give their children four "As":

> **Acceptance: self-worth and security**
> **Appreciation: affirmation and praise**
> **Affection: love and care**
> **Availability: time and attention**

EMPLOYEES AND EMPLOYERS

Paul addressed the roles of three different human relationships in Colossians 3:18–4:1. These Scriptures clearly state how people should respond to those in authority. Workers are to obey their employers. First, Paul told them how. Obedience is to come from the heart. Simple compliance in actions is not enough. Employees are to wil-lingly follow their employers—because of reverence for God. Second, he told employees to work hard. Diligent work is a service to God. In 1 Peter 2:18, employees are instructed to obey all managers, even the harsh or difficult ones. Finally, Paul reminds workers of the rewards
of obedience.

Read the following Scriptures and identify some rewards of submission. Record in the space provided a blessing which comes to believers who follow God's plan for human relationships.

1. 1 Peter 3:1 _____

2. 1 Peter 3:5–6 _____

3. Ephesians 5:32–33 _____

4. Titus 2:3–5 _____

5. 1 Peter 3:4 _____

6. 1 Peter 3:7 _____

Ultimately, the greatest reward for obedience is received by the believer in heaven. People may not always appreciate their efforts, but God will offer eternal rewards to those who follow His pattern for human relationships. What a relief to know that we don't have to please others; we must please God.

Whatever you do, do it heartily, as to the Lord and not to men" (Col. 3:23).

Periodically every Christian needs to examine her heart, especially her attitude about submitting to the authority of others.

How submissive are you to God, your husband (if married), your father (if unmarried), your employer, spiritual leaders, and government officials? Identify three ways you can practice healthy submission to those in authority over you. Write your plans below.

1. _____
   _____

2. _____
   _____

3. _____
   _____

LESSON TEN — THE SPEECH OF A BELIEVER

COLOSSIANS 4:2–6

The Apostle Paul made a significant contribution to Christianity through his missionary journeys and New Testament epistles. He preached, taught, and wrote about some of the most important doctrines of the faith. But do you know what Paul wrote most about? He wrote about behavior. More than anything else, Paul challenged Christians to live godly lives. He believed Christians should act differently than non-Christians—that believers actually became like new persons after conversion.

Behavior is the way a person conducts herself. The actions of a person reflect outwardly whom the person is inside. Thus Paul exhorted Christians to live the life of Christ in the world. In the book of Colossians, Paul first addressed the personal behavior of the believer (Col. 3:5-17). Then he discussed the behavior of Christians at home (Col. 3:18–4:1). In Colossians 4:2–6, he described the verbal behavior of the believer.

Reflect for a moment on Paul's many teachings about behavior.

Romans 12:9–21	*Christian Behavior*
1 Corinthians 13:1–13	*Loving Behavior*
2 Corinthians 7:2–12	*Repentant Behavior*
Galatians 5:22–23	*Fruitful Behavior*
Ephesians 5:22–6:4	*Family Behavior*
Philippians 2:1–11	*Humble Behavior*

Colossians 2:6–10	*Faithful Behavior*
1 Thessalonians 2:1–12	*Paul's Own Behavior*
2 Thessalonians 3:6–15	*Hard Working Behavior*
1 Timothy 3:1–3	*Behavior of Church Leaders*
2 Timothy 1:7–12	*Bold Behavior*
Titus 2:1–8	*Mentoring Behavior*
Philemon 17–22	*Obedient Behavior*

Paul was thorough in his biblical discussion of Christian behavior. He wisely included speech as a behavior for Christians to improve. In several of his letters, Paul discussed the characteristics of godly speech.

Read these verses and write a teaching about the believer's speech.

1 Corinthians 2:6–7 _____

_____

2 Corinthians 12:6 _____

_____

Ephesians 4:15 _____

_____

Ephesians 4:32 _____

_____

Colossians 4:6 _____

_____

Titus 2:15 _____

_____

Speech is a behavior. Fortunately for Christians, speech is a learned behavior. Therefore, it is a behavior that we can change. God calls us to have the speech of a believer. In Colossians 4:2–6, speech is discussed on three levels. Read these verses carefully to understand how Christians are to speak with God, speak of Him, and speak in actions.

SPEAK TO GOD

Paul talked often about the importance of prayer—communication with God. At the very beginning of the book of Colossians, he gave specific ways to pray—lift up others, thank the Father, and ask for power (Col. 1:3–12). He teaches us to pray by example and by instruction in the same way that Jesus did in Matthew 6:5–15.

As Paul moves to the close of his letter to the Christians in Colosse, he reminds them again of the importance of prayer. Twice in Colossians 4:2 he expresses the urgency of prayer when he says "continue earnestly in prayer" and be "vigilant." The believer is to be fervent in prayer—speaking to God continually, faithfully, and passionately.

Read this translation of the same verse: "Devote yourselves to prayer, keeping alert in it with an attitude of thanksgiving" (Col. 4:2, NAS). Now write this verse in your own words._____

_____

_____

_____

_____

Christians are to have active prayer lives, devoting themselves to prayer. The Greek word *proskartere* is translated "devote yourselves" and means "to be steadfast" or "to endure." So an active prayer life is constant, ongoing, continual. Active prayer is alert—always noticing the needs of others. Christians are to be watchful, alert to the needs of the world and the will of God. In a practical way, believers need to find their ideal time to pray when they are alert and fresh.

For many years I struggled with the verse that says "O God, You are my God, early will I seek you" (Psalm 63:1). You see, I'm not a morning person! My husband teases that I don't believe in God until 10:00 A.M. I always respond that I believe in God before 10:00 A.M., I just don't act like it. You can imagine my joy when I discovered this translation of that same verse: "earnestly will I seek you" (Psalm 63:1, NAS). I do want to seek the Lord, but I need to be alert. Early mornings are not best for me. Believers need to find their best time to pray. *That* you pray is more important than *when* you pray.

Finally, Paul says prayer requires an attitude of thanksgiving. Throughout the book of Colossians, the apostle has stressed the importance of a grateful heart. Be grateful for salvation (1:12). Be grateful for spiritual growth (2:6). Be grateful for fellowship with

Christ and His church (3:15). Be grateful for the opportunity to serve (3:17). And be grateful that God answers prayer (4:2-4). These are five excellent "Be Attitudes" about prayer.

I n verses 3 and 4, Paul encourages believers to pray for him and for the others who ministered with him. "Us" in Colossians 4:3 probably refers to Timothy and all Christians in Rome plus the apostle Paul himself. He specifically requested prayer for them as they witnessed. Open doors (opportunities) and a clear word (testimony) are necessary witnessing tools. Prayer is the key that unlocks the door of an unbeliever's heart to the witness of a Christian. Pray that you will speak of Him boldly! Pray for other Christians to be bold witnesses.

While lifestyle evangelism is effective in opening doors to the lost, a verbal witness is essential for the spread of the gospel. Paul not only desired prayer for opportunities, but specifically for opportunities "to speak the mystery of Christ" (Col. 4:3).

Reread Colossians 1:26–27, which addresses the "mystery" of the Old Testament revealed in the New. That mystery which needs to be shared verbally is the gospel—"Christ in you, the hope of glory."

In Colossians 4:6 Paul encourages believers to "season their speech with salt." What does that phrase mean to you? _____

_____

_____

_____

The words of a Christian should be seasoned and well chosen. Salt preserves, purifies, and flavors. The speech of a Christian should have that same effect on the unsaved. Jesus Christ shared His living water with the woman at the well who was spiritually thirsty. He said to her, "whoever drinks of the water that I shall give him will never thirst" (John 4:14). The loving words of a Christian can lead to witness.

Paul's final phrase in Colossians 4:6 reminds believers of the importance of a personal witness. Each believer must be sensitive to the needs of others and depend on the Holy Spirit's guidance to say just the right thing. Fear is the most common obstacle to witnessing. Christians fear inadequacy, rejection, and failure as they speak of Him. In another epistle, Paul reminds us that "God has not given us a spirit of fear, but of power and love and of a sound mind" (2 Tim. 1:7). Remember that the power of the Holy Spirit is with you as you speak the gospel.

SPEAK OF HIM

SPEAK LIKE HIM

Do you agree with this age-old proverb: "actions speak louder than words?" Whether you want to believe it or not, it is true. Your actions overshadow your words. What you do is heard louder than what you say. For the Christian, both the verbal witness and a lifestyle of godliness are necessary if others are to receive the gospel message. If a Christian does not live like Christ, a word of witness will not be effective.

Colossians 4:5 says, "Walk in wisdom toward those who are outside." In other words, behave with wisdom toward unbelievers (see also 1 Cor. 5:12–13; 1 Thess. 4:12; 1 Tim. 3:7). Let's examine the word wisdom to know how to act. Wisdom means "the ability to collect and concisely organize principles from Scripture." The Christian is to live out biblical principles.

In the book of 1 Corinthians, Paul contrasted worldly wisdom and scriptural wisdom.

Read 1 Corinthians 3:18–4:5 then list several characteristics of wisdom below.

Worldly Wisdom	Spiritual Wisdom
1._____	1._____
2._____	2._____
3._____	3._____
4._____	4._____
5._____	5._____

Ask God to give you spiritual wisdom that is reflected in your speech and actions.

Speech is a difficult behavior to control. But God can give us the power to speak to Him, speak of Him, and speak like Him. The behavior of a believer should be Christlike and Christ-pleasing. Psalm 19:14 challenges all believers to discipline their words and thoughts.

Fill your name in the blanks to personalize the pronoun "my." Then pray this prayer to God.

Let the words of_____'s mouth
And the meditation of_____'s heart
Be acceptable in your sight,
O Lord,_____'s strength
and_____'s Redeemer.

59

*L*et your speech always be with grace, seasoned with salt, that you may know how you ought to answer each one" (Col. 4:6).

*I*f actions speak louder than words, perhaps you should carefully examine your actions. Do your actions speak of God and His great love?

Think of three things you have done recently that spoke of God to others. Record them below.

1. _____

2. _____

3. _____

Commit your actions to Him each day.

LESSON ELEVEN — A FOND FAREWELL

COLOSSIANS 4:7–18

The time had come for Paul to bid a fond farewell to the church at Colosse, to Christian friends he had never met. Though he had not visited the Colossians, Paul felt a close kinship with the fellow believers because of his faithful prayers for them. He challenged them to continue in their faith (Col. 4:2–6) and then began his lingering good-bye (Col. 4:7–18). Saying good-bye to ones you love is often hard, especially if you have an important message to communicate.

I always have a hard time saying good-bye to my sister, Mitzi. When we talk on the telephone, our conversation can go on for hours, and we frequently say good-bye a dozen times before we hang up. We always think of one more thing to say, one more question to ask, one more message to pass along. So our good-byes can go on for some time. I understand Paul's hesitation to end his letter. He thought of one more thing to say, one more question to ask, one more message to pass along. But in Colossians 4:18 he finally said "amen," good-bye, the end.

In his opening greeting, Paul identified himself and his intended audience (Col. 1:1–2). Then he extended grace and peace to them from God the Father and the Lord Jesus Christ. As he concluded his letter, Paul identified those companions who had labored for Christ with him (Col. 4:7–14), and he acknowledged more specifically the recipients of his letter (Col. 4:15).

Take time now to read Colossians 4:7–18. List below those co-workers identified by Paul.

1. _____

2. _____

3. _____

4. _____
5. _____
6. _____
7. _____
8. _____
9. _____
10. _____

Paul gave a brief personal introduction of these co-laborers in the book of Colossians; then he expressed closing greetings, and a final blessing. This format is similar to other epistles, a typical Greco-Roman correspondence form with the greeting at the end. However, his style and expression vary somewhat from his other writings. Biblical experts agree that Paul probably wrote this letter about the same time he wrote Philemon (A.D. 60–63). Now let's carefully examine the last few verses of Colossians.

In Colossians 4:7–18, Paul the apostle identified by name ten different believers who ministered with him. Look back at your previous assignment to see if you correctly listed all ten individuals. How did you do? Next we will learn more about these faithful Christians who were acknowledged by Paul in this letter.

PERSONAL INTRODUCTIONS

> *Tychicus* (TIK-ih-kuhs).
> Paul immediately identified a trusted friend and companion, Tychicus.

Read the following passages, then write what you learn about this man of God: Acts 20:1–4; Ephesians 6:21; Colossians 4:7–9; 2 Timothy 4:12; and Titus 3:12 . _____

_____

_____

_____

_____

_____

Tychicus means "fortunate." Indeed, Tychicus was fortunate to serve and minister with Paul. But the apostle was also blessed to have a faithful co-worker. Paul's love for Tychicus was obvious and Tychicus's devotion to Paul and the Lord were evidenced in his actions. He delivered the letter and important information to the Christians in Colosse. He was greatly used by God in building the early church.

Onesimus (oh-NESS-ih-muhs).
> In contrast to the character of Tychicus, Paul mentions another companion, Onesimus, a runaway slave.

Read Colossians 4:9 and Philemon 10–16 before you write a brief description of this Christian friend. _____

_____

_____

_____

_____

Onesimus was apparently the slave of Philemon, a leader in the Colossian church. He ran away to Rome, where Onesimus was led to Christ by Paul. He accompanied Tychicus with the letter from Paul to Colosse. Paul pleaded with Philemon to forgive Onesimus and welcome him back as a new man in Christ.

Aristarchus (er-iss-TAHR-kuhs).
> Little is known from Scripture about Aristarchus. Read these passages in Acts (19:29; 20:4; 27:2) in addition to Colossians 4:10.

What did you learn about Aristarchus? _____

_____

_____

_____

_____

Aristarchus was a Jewish believer from the city of Thessalonica in the region of Macedonia. He was imprisoned in Rome with Paul at the time of this writing. The accounts in the book of Acts record the supportive role Aristarchus played in Paul's ministry. He was a dependable co-laborer, always present when Paul needed him—facing an angry mob (Acts 19:29), returning to Jerusalem (Acts 20:4), or traveling to Rome (Acts 27:4). The ministry of Paul the apostle was strengthened by the faithful efforts of believers like Aristarchus.

Mark (also called John Mark).
> John Mark was with Paul again in Rome. He is truly a complex individual who had returned to minister with Paul.

Read these selected passages and write about this man of renewed faith: 2 Timothy 4:11; Philemon 23–24; 1 Peter 5:13. _____

_____

_____

_____

_____

The cousin of Barnabas, Mark ministered not only with Paul but with Peter and Timothy as well. Mark accompanied Paul and Barnabas on the first missionary journey (Acts 12:25–14:28). However, John Mark left them abruptly and returned to Jerusalem (Acts 13:13). Paul was disappointed with Mark's lack of commitment and later disagreed with Barnabas about his participation in the third missionary journey (Acts 15:36–40). Details about the separation are unclear but Mark returned to serve with Paul. While he didn't actually minister with Jesus, he witnessed much of the work of the early church. He wrote one of the four gospels recording the life and work of Jesus Christ.

> *Justus* (JUHS-tuhs).
> Only one verse in Scripture mentions "Jesus who is called Justus" (Col. 4:11). He is included in Paul's discussion of Jewish believers "who are of the circumcision" (Col. 4:11)— Tychicus, Onesimus, Aristarchus, Mark, and Justus.

Next Paul mentions other Christian workers.

> *Epaphras* (EP-uh-frass).
> Epaphras is the only person mentioned earlier in the book of Colossians.

Read Colossians 1:7 and 4:12–13 then describe this fellow bondservant. _____

_____

_____

_____

_____

Converted during Paul's ministry in Ephesus, Epaphras is apparently the pastor of the Colossian church who is visiting with Paul in Rome. He was instrumental in spreading the gospel to the Lychus Valley and served as a messenger between Paul and the Christians in Colosse. Paul recognized him as a committed prayer warrior. He was a real-life example of one who continually and vigilantly prayed (Col. 4:2).

Luke.
The beloved physician and another writer of the gospels, Luke was with Paul in Rome.

What a host of characters accompanied Paul during his ministry! Read these verses and write a brief description of this familiar man: Colossians 4:14; 2 Timothy 4:11; Philemon 24. _____

_____

_____

_____

_____

_____

Luke was apparently Paul's personal physician and close friend. He frequently traveled with Paul and remained with him as his ministry drew to a close. At times, only Luke was with Paul (2 Tim. 4:11). While little more background is known about Luke, he obviously enjoyed a special relationship with the great apostle.

Demas (DEE-muhs).
Though his name is unfamiliar to many Christians today, Demas was identified by Paul in three of his letters.

Read the following references: Colossians 4:14; 2 Timothy 4:10; Philemon 24. What does the Bible say about Demas? _____

_____

_____

_____

_____

_____

Demas is included in the list of co-laborers with Paul. However, Paul stops short of offering praise for Demas. In 2 Timothy 4:10,

Paul reports that he left his faith: Demas "loved the world." How sad for a child of God to turn to sin! Paul must have had a broken heart. Ministers today are heartbroken when Christians leave the Lord. Pray for those who have left their first love.

Nymphas (NIM-fuhs).
In Colossians 4:15 Paul asks the Colossians to greet other believers— those in Laodicea, Nymphas, and members of his church. Some biblical scholars do not isolate Nymphas as an individual named by Paul as a co-laborer. Other translators identify Nympha as a female (see Col. 4:15, RSV). What Scripture does say is that a church or body of believers was meeting together in Nymphas's home. All New Testament churches met in homes (for example, Acts 12:12; Rom. 16:5; 1 Cor. 16:19; Philemon 2). Paul sent greetings to Nymphas and the church members there.

Archippus (ahr-KIP-uhs).
At the end of this letter, Paul mentions a final Christian brother, Archippus. His name appears only in Colossians 4:17 and Philemon 2.

What do these verses tell you about Archippus? _____

_____

_____

_____

_____

_____

_____

Archippus undoubtedly was a faithful believer. He was an active member of the church that met in Philemon's home (Philemon 2). Archippus may have been the son of Philemon and Apphia. The verse in Colossians (v. 17) records Paul's exhortation to young Archippus to remain faithful to his call to ministry. Because of the disobedience of Demas, Paul reminded Archippus and all Christians of the need for persistent obedience.

In the final section of Colossians, Paul identifies Christian companions and co-laborers. Then, he expresses his closing greetings. Initially Paul sends greetings from those ministering with him.

CLOSING
GREETINGS

66

- Aristarchus, with Mark and Justus (Col. 4:10)
- Epaphras (Col. 4:12)
- Luke and Demas (Col. 4:14)

Then Paul asks the Colossians to greet specific individuals (see Col. 4:15).

- brethren in Laodicea
- Nymphas
- the members of the church at Nymphas's house.

What do you think is the purpose of the greeting in a New Testament letter? _____

_____

_____

Did Paul accomplish the purpose in his epistle to the Colossians?

_____

Explain. _____

_____

_____

_____

What is an epistle? _____

_____

_____

In a recent cartoon strip, an epistle was defined as "the New Testament version of email." Certainly, the word *epistle* is not used very often in daily conversation today. But Christians should be familiar with this biblical term.

An epistle is an instructive letter. The Bible includes many letters—some are mentioned in Bible books, while others are the entire book of the Bible. More than half of the New Testament books are epistles. The apostle Paul wrote 13 of the New Testament letters which are often referred to as Pauline Epistles. In another comic strip, a young boy asks his Sunday School teacher, "How did Paul send his letters—by regular mail, Fed Ex, or email?" Obviously Paul's letters were delivered personally by Christian friends. Sending letters was the primary form of communication for the early church.

The personal introductions and closing greeting are followed by Paul's final blessing. Before you read Colossians 4:18, reread Colossians 1:2. Paul opens and closes this letter to the Colossian Christians the same way. He extends to them "grace" from God.

Paul's final blessing was the same in all of his epistles. Read each biblical reference below, then fill in the blank to complete Paul's blessing to his Christian friends.

Romans 16:24 "The _____ of our Lord Jesus Christ be with you all."

1 Corinthians 16:23–24 "The _____ of the Lord Jesus Christ be with you. My _____ be with you all in Christ Jesus."

2 Corinthians 13:14 "The _____ of the Lord Jesus Christ, and the _____ of God, and the _____ of the Holy Spirit be with you all."

Galatians 6:18 "The _____ of our Lord be with your spirit."

Ephesians 6:24 "_____ be with all those who love our Lord Jesus Christ in sincerity."

Philippians 4:23 "The _____ of our Lord Jesus Christ be with you all."

Colossians 4:18 "_____ be with you."

1 Thessalonians 5:28 "The _____ of our Lord Jesus Christ be with you."

2 Thessalonians 3:18 "The _____ of our Lord Jesus Christ be with you all."

1 Timothy 6:21 "_____ be with you."

2 Timothy 4:22 "_____ be with you."

Titus 3:15 "_____ be with you all."

Philemon 25 "The _____ of our Lord Jesus Christ be with your spirit."

While Paul occasionally added to his final blessing, he always extended grace to those Christians who received his letter.

Why do you think "grace" was always the last word uttered by Paul?

_____

Salvation by grace through faith was the primary message of Paul's ministry and writings. Once and for all, he wanted Christians to understand that salvation was by faith and not works, the gracious gift of the Lord Jesus Christ. Paul had found God's grace to be sufficient for all his needs. He frequently emphasized in his closing that grace was for "all." He dispelled the belief that only the Jewish people were chosen for salvation. God's grace is for all—the Jew and the Greek, male and female. What an amazing grace gift from God!

*T*ake heed to the ministry which you have received in the Lord, that you may fulfill it" (Col. 4:17).

Toward what ministry has God called you?

Prayerfully read the "Prescription 11 for Wellness" above (Col. 4:17). Have you been faithful to the ministry you have received from the Lord? Hear Paul's exhortation to fellow ministers, then write a prayer of recommitment to be a faithful minister of God.

_____
_____
_____
_____
_____

CONCLUSION

You have now completed this study of the book of Colossians written by the apostle Paul. You have considered many different topics. You have discovered many biblical truths. You have concentrated on several doctrines. But overall, you have focused on faith and fitness. Now you may be better able to answer the question, How can Christians stay spiritually fit? The book of Colossians is truly "A Woman's Guide to Spiritual Wellness."

Many Christians place themselves at risk spiritually when they don't strengthen their faith. A weak Christian is vulnerable to spiritual illness in the same way that a frail person is susceptible to physical illness. For years, the medical field was focused on sickness—eliminating or treating disease. But now, doctors are most concerned about the total wellness of their patients. They emphasize prevention and healthy lifestyles. Wellness is "a dynamic process of improving one's health status at any phase or in any dimension of health." Wellness affects the whole person.

The Bible advocates spiritual wellness. Christians should not wait for spiritual illness to occur and treat it. Instead, growing Christians must work to prevent spiritual decline and alter their lifestyles to promote total wellness. Paul discussed well being in 1 Thessalonians 5:23:

> **"Now may the God of peace Himself sanctify you entirely [or wholly]; and may your spirit and soul and body be preserved complete, without blame at the coming of our Lord Jesus Christ" (NASB).**

God desires His children to be wholly holy until He comes again.

In the book of Colossians, Paul taught many biblical truths that you can practice to develop your spiritual wellness.

Reflect back on these basic teachings which should influence a believer's daily life.

Prayer Pleases God	Colossians 1:1–12
Christ is God Incarnate, the Only Way to Salvation	Colossians 1:13–23
Christians Should Rejoice in Suffering	Colossians 1:24–29
Believers are Built Up in Christ	Colossians 2:1–15
Christians Should Add Nothing to Faith	Colossians 2:16–23
The Christian Life is Set Apart	Colossians 3:1–11
Christians Must Put on Love	Colossians 3:12–17
Christians Must Be Submissive as Unto the Lord	Colossians 3:18–4:1
Believers Must Speak Like Christ	Colossians 4:2–6

Tommy Yessick, a wellness expert with the Baptist Sunday School Board of the Southern Baptist Convention, suggests that there are six dimensions of wellness: emotional, intellectual, occupational, physical, social, and spiritual. Let's review Colossians to see what the apostle Paul had to say about each dimension of wellness. As you read each passage, be sure to examine your own personal health. A Christian cannot be spiritually well unless she is healthy emotionally, intellectually, occupationally, physically, and socially, as well as spiritually.

EMOTIONAL WELL-BEING

Emotional well-being is perceived by mental health professionals to be the stabilizing factor for all the other wellness dimensions. God created humans as emotional beings, with feelings and attitudes. He desires for His children to have a passion for Him and deep feelings for others. Emotions are a person's way to express the feelings within. Women are especially emotional creatures. The experiences of life bring pain or joy, sadness, or anger for a woman. Healthy emotional well-being bonds believers to God and to each other in deep relationships.

Paul freely expressed his emotions in his letters to Christians of the early church. He voiced feelings of love, concern, and understanding. In Colossians 2:1–3, Paul's passionate feelings for the Christians in Colosse were obvious. Read that passage of Scripture, then list some of the emotions experienced by Paul.

_____

_____

- "I have a great conflict for you"
- "your hearts may be encouraged"
- "being knit together in love"

I am a very emotional person. In fact, I cry often, whether I am happy or sad, refreshed or fatigued, agreeable or angry. I have often asked the Lord to dry up my tears. But He always reminds me of His tender heart. I do want to have a heart like His—a heart of compassion and care and concern. A tender heart is a tearful heart. So get out the tissues, friends. Now I just ask the Lord to help me control my tears so that my words of witness can be understood clearly.

INTELLECTUAL WELL-BEING

Intellectual or mental well-being is the human's ability to think, to learn, and to explore and understand information. The human mind is an amazing creation of God. With our minds, we can reason, have opinions, acquire knowledge, increase awareness, and sharpen perception. It is important, however, for Christians to guard their minds from evil and use their mental powers for good. Intellectual well-being requires the believer to be alert, rational, and sensible.

In Colossians 2:8–10, Paul warns the Colossians to protect their minds from false teachings. Many Christians were believing and following the principles of the world. The apostle attempted to proclaim the truth so Christians could detect deception. Heresy distorts truth and distracts the believer.

In Colossians, Paul describes heresy as persuasive (2:4), traditional (2:8), legalistic (2:16), mystical (2:18), and intellectual (2:23). Contrast human heresy and biblical truth. _____

_____

_____

_____

_____

_____

Christians can deflect heresy when you "set your mind on things above, not on things on the earth" (Col. 3:2).

Josh McDowell is a well-known Christian speaker and writer. Years ago, as a young agnostic, Josh set out to disprove God by reading the Bible. As he read Scripture, he heard the truth and his own human philosophy faltered. He was converted to faith in Jesus Christ as he read the Bible. Today he is recognized as a leading Christian in apologetics, the defense of the faith.

When God created the first people, He had a job for them—care for the creatures of the earth (Gen. 1:26–27). All humans are created for a purpose. Without a purpose or a job to do, one has little reason to live. Paul challenges believers do the work of God, to be His hands and feet in proclaiming the message of salvation. Occupational well-being results when an individual loves her work. Satisfaction in work, excellence in performance, and continued professional growth contribute to overall health and wellness.

Paul addressed the subject of occupational well-being in Colossians 1:24–29. He specifically discussed his own "call to ministry and the calling of others to full-time Christian service. Paul even viewed his physical sufferings as a part of his work for the Lord. His call was from God and for the preaching of His Word (Col. 1:25). The apostle fulfilled his call to ministry with great zeal. Whether in full-time ministry or a secular career, Christians today are called by God for a purpose. When we hear that call and understand its purpose, we should work diligently and excel professionally.

How did Paul say he worked? Read Colossians 1:29 then write the answer here._____

_____

_____

_____

_____

For fifteen years I worked as director of speech pathology in a large medical center. I was called to that work, and I loved it. Then God gave me a new call—He called me to full-time ministry as a Christian speaker, teacher, and writer. I love my new work too! Why? I love it because I am in the will of God for my life. When Christians are doing the will of God in their work, they will experience occupational wellness.

OCCUPATIONAL WELL-BEING

74

PHYSICAL WELL-BEING

The human body is a complex machine created perfectly by God to function smoothly. In order to function, the body must be cared for —proper physical maintenance is essential to efficient performance. For the believer, care of the body is a biblical mandate. The body is the temple of the Lord—His dwelling place. As a steward of that temple, the Christian should care for herself both spiritually and physically.

While legalistic observation of rituals is not necessary for salvation, the believer should be a good steward of what is taken into the body. Proper nutrition and regular exercise are essential to physical well-being.

There are several wonderful biblically-based weight-control programs today like First Place, Weigh Down Workshop, and Faithfully Fit. Spiritual discipline is emphasized in concert with physical discipline. A Christian can grow spiritually while learning to control her diet. A biblical approach to weight control and regular exercise leads to physical wellness.

SOCIAL WELL-BEING

Social well-being includes healthy relationships and a viable support network. The family unit is the first context for development of social skills—learning to relate to people in a happy, positive way. Friends also provide nurturing relationships. For the Christian, the church family can be a source of deep friendships. Every human being has a desire to belong to a group that gives love and support and affirmation. Social well-being cannot be developed in isolation. People must get together, form connections, and build relationships. Many strong personal relationships last a lifetime and promote overall success.

Paul reminded the church in Colosse about the new character of the believer. In Colossians 3:12–14, he stated that new belief results in new behavior. Christians should treat people differently.

Read Colossians 3:12–14 and describe how believers should relate to other people. _____

_____

_____

_____

Love, patience, and forgiveness should characterize the life of the Christian. When you show love to others, they will love in return. Godly behavior strengthens interpersonal relationships.

I love people! When given a choice, I would always choose to be in a room full of people than alone. My husband is the exact opposite.

He is happiest when he is alone with a book. Whether you are a social butterfly or a recluse, you must work to improve your social relationships. My husband has worked diligently to improve his social skills because of his call to ministry. Christians can have a powerful influence on other people as they demonstrate acceptance, affirmation, and affection. Those social skills come directly from God.

Faith in God and a personal relationship with Jesus Christ are key ingredients to spiritual well-being. Head knowledge without heartfelt passion does not create a healthy Christian. Instead, a Christian must have a personal faith which grows daily through Bible study, prayer, witnessing, and ministry. No one else can secure a believer's spiritual health. Every Christian must grow in faith and live out that faith in her daily life. The spiritual well-being of every Christian is God's greatest desire, but spiritual vitality will not become a reality without wellness in all dimensions of life.

In Colossians 2:6–7, Paul clearly stated the prescription for spiritual well-being: "As you therefore have received Christ Jesus the Lord so walk in Him, rooted and built up in Him and established in the faith."

What does that Scripture teach you about spiritual wellness? _____

_____

_____

_____

_____

I hear Paul's challenge to live a committed life—dependent on God, not on myself or others, and confident in His presence and His provision.

As you conclude this study of Colossians, I pray that you are healthier and stronger spiritually now than you were when you began the study. Paul did his part to promote your spiritual wellness in his writing of this powerful book. I have tried to do my part to encourage your spiritual wellness as I directed your study of God's Word and shared my personal insights. Now it's your turn to live out what you have learned about spiritual wellness. You can do it with the help of God!

Always remember that fitness, like faith, is a journey not a destination. And God's prescriptions in His Word are the only guarantee of good health. Be assured of my prayers for you as you live a healthy, happy Christian life!

PRESCRIPTION 12
FOR SPIRITUAL
WELLNESS

PERSONAL
SPIRITUAL
WELLNESS

*T*o them God willed to make known what are the riches of the glory of the mystery among the Gentiles: which is Christ in you, the hope of glory" (Col. 1:27).

*A*t this time, evaluate your overall health and wellness. How fit are you? Regardless of the answer, every Christian should strive for greater well-being.

Set at least one personal goal for wellness in each area listed below.

Emotional well-being _____

Intellectual well-being _____

Occupational well-being _____

Physical well-being _____

Social well-being _____

Spiritual well-being _____

Now make the commitment to accomplish these goals with the help of the Lord.

12 PRESCRIPTIONS FOR SPIRITUAL WELLNESS

1. *G*race to you and peace from God our Father
   and the Lord Jesus Christ" (Col. 1:2*b*).

2. *W*alk worthy of the Lord, fully pleasing Him, being fruitful in every
   good work and increasing in the knowledge of God" (Col. 1:10).

3. *H*e is the image of the invisible God, the firstborn
   over all creation" (Col. 1:15).

4. *T*o this end I also labor, striving according to His working which
   works in me mightily" (Col. 1:29).

5. *A*s you therefore have received Christ Jesus the Lord,
   so walk in Him" (Col. 2:6).

6. *T*herefore, if you died with Christ from the basic principles of the world, why, as
   though living in the world, do you subject yourselves to regulations?" (Col. 2:20).

7. *S*et your mind on things above, not on things
   on the earth" (Col. 3:2).

8. *B*ut above all these things put on love, which is the
   bond of perfection" (Col. 3:14).

9. *W*hatever you do, do it heartily, as to the
   Lord and not to men" (Col. 3:23).

10. *L*et your speech always be with grace, seasoned with
    salt, that you may know how you ought to answer each one" (Col. 4:6).

11. *T*ake heed to the ministry which you have received in the
    Lord, that you may fulfill it" (Col. 4:17).

12. *T*o them God willed to make known what are the riches of the glory of the
    mystery among the Gentiles: which is Christ in you, the hope of
    glory" (Col. 1:27).

This section includes some teaching suggestions for the small group leader. It also provides a format for the discussion time and a typical schedule for a one-hour session. A focus group has tried this particular approach, and it was successful. Let the Holy Spirit lead your group discussion, and make any appropriate changes. These are simply teaching helps.

LESSON ONE: CALLED BY CHRIST

Prayer Time (5 minutes)

Ask each member of the group to write a prayer of commitment in the front of her Bible study book. Spend a few minutes in personal prayer, asking God to bless this Bible study.

Review (5 minutes)

Discuss the format for this study and details about the group meeting. Encourage each member to complete her own study before discussing it with the group.

Scripture Reading (5 minutes)

Read Colossians 1:1–2 aloud. Suggest that members circle the name of the author of this book and underline any description of him.

Group Discussion (40 minutes)

1. Discuss the medical field's focus on wellness and the Christian's need for spiritual wellness.

2. Talk about the author of Colossians. Ask the following questions:
   - Who wrote the book of Colossians? (Paul)
   - Who was with him? (Timothy)
   - What do you know about Paul's birth, rebirth, life, journeys, writings, and death?

3. Briefly discuss the audience receiving this letter from Paul.

   - the city
   - the church
   - the conflict

Refer to a map of Paul's missionary journeys.

4. Discuss Paul's admonition to the church of Colosse—his warning.

5. Review Paul's answers—the three central themes of the book of Colossians

Closing (5 minutes)

1. Read "Prescription 1 for Spiritual Wellness" (Col. 1:26) aloud as a group

2. Share personal insights about who you are in Christ.

Prayer Time (5 minutes)

Give out index cards to each member and ask her to record one specific prayer request. Collect the cards, then distribute one card to each person. Pray silently for that particular need.

Review (5 minutes)

Review Lesson One by asking the following questions:

Who wrote Colossians?
Why was it written?
Where was it written?

LESSON TWO:
PRAYER PLEASES
GOD

What are its themes?
To whom was it written?

Scripture Reading (5 minutes)

Ask a volunteer to read Colossians 1:1–12 aloud. Encourage all members to underline any instructions about prayer in this passage of Scripture.

Group Discussion (40 minutes)

1. Ask the question, "Why do you think prayer pleases God?"

2. Introduce this lesson by stating Paul's three specific ways to pray: lift up others, thank the Father, and ask for power.

3. Discuss Paul's guidelines for praying for others from Colossians 1:1–12.

4. Compare and contrast these types of prayer: petition and intercession.

5. Encourage members to share praises to God and thanksgiving for His blessings.

6. Answer this question as a group: "Why is it important for Christians to ask God for power?"

Closing (5 minutes)

1. Go around the room and have each member read aloud one word of "Prescription 2 for Spiritual Wellness" (Col. 1:10). Then read the entire passage aloud.

2. Quietly reread your prayer of commitment recorded in "Personal Spiritual Wellness."

3. Share the closing salutation of Colossians with someone in the group: "Grace to you and peace from God our Father and the Lord Jesus Christ."

Prayer Time (5 minutes)

Read chorally "A Hymn of Him" from Colossians 1:15–20 as a prayer. The leader should read the verses and the entire group read the chorus.

Review (5 minutes)

Review Lesson Two by asking: "What did Paul teach us about prayer?" Then ask, "What have you personally learned about prayer this week?

Scripture Reading (5 minutes)

Ask one member of the group to read the entire focal passage aloud: Colossians 1:13–23.

Group Discussion (40 minutes)

1. Define "Christology" and briefly discuss its importance to the Christian.

2. Ask the members to name some of the descriptors of Christ found in Colossians 1:13–23.

3. Discuss the fact that Christ is fully God and fully man. Refer to several Scripture references in this lesson.

4. Rejoice together as you share specific creations of God.

5. Answer this question as a group: "What does the Bible teach about Christ as Head of the church?"

6. Discuss "reconciliation" and how Christ reconciles the world.

Closing (5 minutes)

1. Read "Prescription 3 for Spiritual Wellness" (Col. 1:15) aloud as a group, slowly and deliberately.

2. Ask members to relate how Christ makes Himself known to them on a daily basis.

Prayer Time (5 minutes)

Follow this model for prayer as you voice sentence prayers to the Father.

> A - adoration
> C - confession
> T - thanksgiving
> S - supplication

Review (5 minutes)

Review Lesson Three's teachings about Christ as you ask these questions:

> Who is Christ?
> What did He create?
> What is His relationship to the church?
> How does He reconcile us to the Father?
> Why is Christ incomparable?

Scripture Reading (5 minutes)

If you have access to *The Message*, read Colossians 1:24–29 in that modern paraphrase. Paul's perspective on suffering is very clear in this passage.

Group Discussion (40 minutes)

1. Briefly discuss three challenges Christians experience: human suffering, the mysteries of the faith, and the call to service.

2. Ask the group: "Do you believe that suffering is experienced by Christians today?" Review Paul's five reasons to rejoice in suffering.

3. Discuss the mystery of the faith. Are there specific things that you don't understand about God? What?

4. Ask several members of the group to share their calls to ministry.

5. Conclude the discussion by asking: "Why should Christians work so hard for the gospel?"

Closing (5 minutes)

1. Read "Prescription 4 for Spiritual Wellness" (Col. 1:29) aloud, then ask several members to restate the verse.

2. Have members pray about their own commitments to proclaiming the gospel.

Prayer Time (5 minutes)

Ask members to pray in "prayer triplets" (groups of three). Pray specifically for each person to be "built up in Christ."

Review (5 minutes)

Review the summary points of Lesson Four: human suffering, the mysteries of the faith, and the call to service. Did anyone complete her gospel "to-do" list this week? Ask members to share what they learned.

Scripture Reading (5 minutes)

Ask five people to read the focal Scripture by section:

(1) Colossians 2:1–3;
(2) Colossians 2:4–5;
(3) Colossians 2:6–7;
(4) Colossians 2:8–10;
(5) Colossians 2:11–15.

Group Discussion (40 minutes)

1. Begin the discussion by asking, "What does it mean to be built up in Christ?"

2. Discuss how Christians should run the race. Read Philippians 3:12–14.

3. List the six verbs from Colossians 2:1–7 on the board—know, encourage, knit, say, receive, walk. Discuss what these verbs teach about being "rooted in Christ."

4. Ask members to paraphrase Colossians 2:8, Paul's warning to believers.

5. Briefly discuss the ordinance of baptism, including ways to celebrate with new converts.

6. Challenge the group to practice biblical forgiveness as taught by Paul in Colossians 2:13–14.

Closing (5 minutes)

1. Read "Prescription 5 for Spiritual Wellness" (Col. 2:6), then ask members to suggest verbs to replace "walk" (example: so *live* in Him, so *talk* in Him, etc.).

2. How spiritually strong is your group? Ask each member to write her total spiritual weight from the Spiritual Wellness activity on a piece of paper that is passed around. Add up the score and announce it. Then pray that God will strengthen the members individually and collectively as a group.

LESSON SIX: THE DIET PRINCIPLE

Prayer Time (5 minutes)

Spend time praying these Scriptures from the book of Colossians. Read each verse aloud then allow time for silent prayer:

Colossians 1:2b, 1:9, 1:12, 2:6,7,4:17–18, 1:3, 1:10,11, 1:24, 4:2

Review (5 minutes)

Draw a tree on the board as you review Lesson Five. Ask this question: "How can you be rooted in Him?"

Scripture Reading (5 minutes)

Ask each person to silently read Colossians 2:16–23 as you begin your discussion of this passage.

Group Discussion (40 minutes)

1. Ask if anyone has ever experienced "the diet principle."

2. Turn in your Bibles to Leviticus 11–15 and skim these chapters in order to mention some of the Jewish regulations. Note how many very specific rules they had to follow.

3. Discuss what the people in Colosse added to faith (asceticism, observances, visions, angels).

4. Compare and contrast what is meant by a "guru" and a "mentor." How have mentors positively influenced your lives?

5. Review these false teachings: half truths, false humility, sinful pride, and unnecessary slavery.

6. Ask members to explain the difference between salvation by faith and salvation by works.

Closing (5 minutes)

1. Ask one member of the group to read "Prescription 6 for Spiritual Wellness" (Col. 2:20).

2. In conclusion, have another person read Galatians 2:18–21 for comparison.

Prayer Time (5 minutes)

Write the following topics on index cards and give to six members of the group: Praise to God, Members of Bible Study Group, The Church, Christian Friends, Unsaved Friends, Thanksgiving to God. Ask each one to voice a topical sentence prayer.

Review (5 minutes)

Review Lesson Six briefly by asking these questions:
1. What are "additives to faith?"
2. What is "the diet guru?"

LESSON SEVEN:
HEALTHY
CHRISTIAN
LIVING

Scripture Reading (5 minutes)

Divide the group into three smaller groups. Ask each small group to read and briefly discuss one of the following Scripture passages: Colossians 3:1–4; Colossians 3:5–7; Colossians 3:8–14.

Group Discussion (40 minutes)

1. Discuss the dangers of legalism of the law (Col. 2:20) and forgiveness of God (Col. 3:2).

2. Ask the group to share some things they worry about, then read Philippians 4:6.

3. Review these three helpful hints about healthy Christian living: be consistent, be real, be godly.

4. Summarize what several New Testament Scriptures teach about the wrath of God.

5. List on the board what behaviors Christians are to "put off" (Col. 3:8-9) and "put on" (Col. 3:12–14).

6. Conclude the discussion by completing the Scripture statements about healthy Christian living.

Closing (5 minutes)

1. Ask each member to silently study "Prescription 7 for Spiritual Wellness" (Col. 3:2), then recite it from memory as a group.

2. Review the six previous "Prescriptions for Spiritual Wellness."

Prayer Time (5 minutes)

Ask each person to find a prayer partner and spend time praying in this manner: Praise to God, Petition for Others, Prayer for Self.

Review (5 minutes)

Review Lesson Seven before you begin this study. Pose this question: "Why is it important for Christians to be consistent, to be real, and to be godly?"

Scripture Reading (5 minutes)

Ask a volunteer in the group to read Colossians 3:12–17 aloud.

Group Discussion (40 minutes)

1. As a group, brainstorm items of clothing they would want to take on a trip. Write the clothing on the board. Use the process of elimination to decide on only eight items.

2. Review the suggested eight-piece wardrobe in this lesson.

3. Discuss the Christian's spiritual wardrobe: tender mercies, kindness, humility, meekness, longsuffering, tolerance, forgiveness, and love.

4. Ask why love is the essential virtue of Christian living.

5. Read Ephesians 6:13–18, then discuss the Christian's wardrobe for spiritual warfare.

6. Complete your discussion by asking: "How do you personally resist spiritual warfare?"

Closing (5 minutes)

1. Call on members of the group to read "Prescription 8 for Spiritual Wellness" (Col. 3:14) in as many different translations of the Bible as represented among the group.

2. Ask individuals to call out specific behaviors that Christians

should "take off" and "put on" that they recorded for this week's "Personal Spiritual Wellness."

LESSON NINE: A SUBMISSIVE HEART

Prayer Time (5 minutes)

Begin this group session with a directed quiet time. Ask members to pray silently following this model written on the board:
Praise to God
Confession of Sin
Requests for Self (physical needs, mental needs, spiritual needs)
Confidence in God

Review (5 minutes)

Review Lesson Eight—the believer's personal wardrobe and spiritual wardrobe. Ask members if they cleaned their spiritual wardrobes this week. What behaviors did they alter?

Scripture Reading (5 minutes)

Have three members of the group read a section of the Scripture focus aloud: Colossians 3:18–19; Colossians 3:20–21; Colossians 3:22–4:1.

Group Discussion (40 minutes)

1. Pose this question as you begin today's lesson: "Who has authority in your life?"

2. Ask members to share their definitions of biblical submission.

3. Fill in the blanks together to complete God's design for human relationships (Col. 3:18–4:1).

4. Discuss how wives submit to their husbands (see Eph. 5:33).

5. Discuss how children submit to parents.

6. Discuss how employees submit to employers.

Closing (5 minutes)

1. Read "Prescription 9 for Spiritual Wellness" (Col. 3:23) aloud, then discuss why it is important to do everything "heartily."

2. Encourage each member to draw a heart in the Bible study book and write this prayer of commitment in it: "Lord, I submit my heart to You and to all people in authority over me."

Prayer Time (5 minutes)

As members come in, ask them to turn in their Bibles to Psalm 23 and spend some time meditating on this prayer of David.

Review (5 minutes)

Review Paul's teaching about submission in human relationships from Lesson Nine: wives to husbands, children to parents, employees to employers.

Scripture Reading (5 minutes)

Ask members to underline in their Bibles the words *prayer*, *speak*, and *walk* as you read aloud Colossians 4:2–6.

Group Discussion (40 minutes)

1. Reflect for a moment on the many teachings by Paul about behavior.

2. Discuss why Paul was so concerned about the behavior of Christians.

3. Ask: "What does Paul teach about prayer in Colossians 4:2–6?"

4. Ask: "Why must Christians speak of Him?"

5. Ask: "How do Christians speak of Him in actions?"

6. Discuss the difference between worldly wisdom and spiritual wisdom.

Closing (5 minutes)

1. Write "Prescription 10 for Spiritual Wellness" (Col. 4:6) on the board substituting "my"/ "your" and "I"/ "you" (two times). Read it aloud together.

2. Ask members to suggest words of kindness that can "season their speech with salt."

LESSON ELEVEN: A FOND FAREWELL

Prayer Time (5 minutes)

For today's prayer time, repeat "The Lord's Prayer" (Matt. 6:9–13) aloud together, slowly and prayerfully.

Review (5 minutes)

Review Lesson Ten, "The Speech of a Believer." Discuss how Christians should speak to God, speak of Him, and speak like Him.

Scripture Reading (5 minutes)

Ask the group to read Colossians 4:7–18 silently and circle the names of all co-workers in ministry mentioned by Paul.

Group Discussion (40 minutes)

1. Briefly describe the format of typical Greco-Roman correspondence.

2. Ask the group to help you list on the board the ten co-workers identified by Paul in Colossians 4:7–18. Practice pronouncing their names correctly.

3. Discuss each individual identified by Paul in his introductions.

4. Underline the names of those individuals listed on the board who actually ministered with Paul.

5. Suggest definitions of an "epistle."

6. Consider why Paul concludes his letters with "grace."

Closing (5 minutes)

1. Ask members to meditate for a few minutes on "Prescription 11 for Spiritual Wellness" (Col. 4:17).

2. Conclude today's study by reading aloud Paul's closing exhortations and blessing in Colossians 4:16–18.

Prayer Time (5 minutes)

Today's opening prayer will be for unbelievers. Ask each person to write down the name of one unsaved friend, then spend some time praying for their spiritual wellness.

Review (5 minutes)

Review the names of the ten individuals mentioned by Paul in Lesson Eleven (Col. 4:7–18). Briefly describe who they were.

Scripture Reading (5 minutes)

Ask six volunteers to read these selected Scriptures from the book of Colossians: Colossians 1:24–29; Colossians 2:1–3; Colossians 2:6–7; Colossians 2:8–10; Colossians 2:16–23; and Colossians 3:12–14.

LESSON TWELVE: FAITH AND FITNESS (CONCLUSION)

Group Discussion (40 minutes)

1. Reflect back over the teachings in Colossians which should influence a believer's daily life (see Lesson Twelve).

2. Ask someone to read 1 Thessalonians 5:23 from the New American Standard Bible, then discuss what Paul meant by "wellness."

3. Draw a circle on the board and divide it into six equal parts then label each section as follows: emotional, intellectual, occupational, physical, social, spiritual.

4. Discuss each aspect of a Christian's well-being.

5. Share practical ways for Christians to maintain wellness in each area.

Closing (5 minutes)

1. Read aloud together "Prescription 12 for Spiritual Wellness" (Col. 1:27), a theme verse in the book of Colossians.

2. Ask members to share the "Prescription for Spiritual Wellness" that has meant the most to them personally.

This section will provide specific answers to direct questions in each lesson. The responses were compiled from Scripture and other biblical sources. Some of the questions solicit personal perspective, so there is no one correct answer. These answers are not included. A key is provided to give you additional insights into the book of Colossians.

LESSON ONE: CALLED BY CHRIST

Who wrote Colossians?
Paul

Who was with him?
Timothy

Had he visited Colosse?
No; "many have not seen my face in the flesh" (Col. 2:1).

Who was Paul the man?
A Jew, converted dramatically, faithful Christian, started churches, wrote 13 letters in the New Testament

How does Paul describe himself in Colossians 1:1 and 1:23?
Paul, "an apostle of Jesus Christ" and "a minister."

Preconversion:
circumcised Jew, legalistic Pharisee, persecuted the church, obedient to law (Phil. 3:3–6)

Postconversion:
an apostle of Christ and a minister of the gospel (Col. 1:1,23).

Paul's salvation testimony:
Jewish leader who persecuted Christians, converted along the Damascus road, blinded by God, sight restored by his faith and with help of Ananias, began preaching and teaching

Colossian Christians:
Saints, faithful, qualified to be partakers of the inheritance of the saints, once alienated but now reconciled, God willed to make known the mystery to the Gentiles (Col. 1:2, 12, 21, 27)

Warning to Christians in Colossians 2:8–10?
Beware of heresy, it will cheat you and deceive you, don't listen to men or the world but to Christ

Reading a letter aloud:
Holds attention, gives expression, becomes memorable

Paul's prayer:
"Grace" and "peace." "Grace" is God's gracious gift of love and salvation, while "peace" is His gift of well-being and fulfillment despite personal circumstances.

Guidelines for praying
Colossians   1:3 - *pray for others at all times*
                      1:9 - *ask that God give His knowledge*
                      1:10 - *ask that they walk worthy*
                      1:11 - *ask that they be strengthened*
                      1:12 - *thank God that they belong to Him*

Petition:
specific requests to God for self

Intercession:
prayer for others

Paul's thanks in Colossians 1:12:
He is thankful for the inheritance of the saints, specifically the inheritance of the gospel and God's kingdom.

LESSON TWO: PRAYER PLEASES GOD

Qualities of Christ (Col. 1:13–23):

deliverer	*creator*
redeemer	*ruler*
forgiver	*eternal*
God	*head of church*
firstborn	*reconciler*

Who created the world?
God made all things (John 1:3).
God made all things (Col 1:16).
God made all the worlds (Heb. 1:2).

The creation (Genesis 1–2):
Day 1 = He created light.
Day 2 = He created land.
Day 3 = He created seas and grass.
Day 4 = He created stars, sun, moon.
Day 5 = He created animals and birds.
Day 6 = He created man.
Day 7 = He rested.

Paul's words to Christians about the church (1 Cor. 12:12-27):
*One body, many members, in Christ, all members necessary to
the whole body, care for each member, one suffers then all suffer,
one honored all honored, body of Christ*

Reconciliation:
Renewal of friendship; harmonizing of apparently opposed ideas

Reconciler:
God ("by Him," Col. 1:20)

Reconciled to whom?
To Him

Result of Reconciliation:
Forgiveness, salvation

How should Christians respond to suffering?
Count it joy, develop patience, complete the faith

All statements about the mysteries of the faith are TRUE.

Christians "To-Do List" (Col. 1:28):
1. *preach Him*
2. *warn every man*
3. *teach every man*

Why?
"That we may present every man perfect in Christ Jesus"
(Col. 1:28).

How Christians should "run the race" (Phil. 3:12–14):
Keep running, press on, keep apprehending, forget past failures, look to the future, keep pressing toward the goal of Jesus

Verbs about faith (Col. 2:1–7):
know = *have information*
encourage = *promote faith in others*
knit = *bring together in love*
say = *speak of faith*
receive = *hear from God*
walk = *live faith through words and deeds*

Teachings about forgiveness (Col. 2):
verse 13 - *all sin is forgiven*
verse 14 - *Christ erased the penalty of sin*
verse 14 - *He carried our sin away, out of sight*

False Teachings in Colossians 2:16–23:
1. *asceticism - verses 16, 21*
2. *observances of days - verse 16*
3. *special visions - verse 18*
4. *worship of angels - verses 18, 20*

Guru:
a human leader who seeks personal attention

Mentor:
a Christlike individual who focuses attention on God

LESSON FIVE: BUILT UP IN CHRIST

LESSON SIX: THE DIET PRINCIPLE

LESSON SEVEN: HEALTHY CHRISTIAN LIVING

Biblical teachings about God's wrath:

John 3:36 - *the unsaved will experience the wrath of God*

Romans 1:18 - *God's wrath is unleashed on ungodlly, unrighteous men*

Romans 2:5 - *hardness of heart and continual sin receive God's wrath*

1 Thessalonians 1:10 - *God's wrath is just and blameless*

Colossians 3:8–14

Put Off	**Put On**
1. anger	*1. tender mercies*
2. wrath	*2. kindness*
3. malice	*3. humility*
4. blasphemy	*4. meekness*
5. filthy language	*5. longsuffering*
6. lying	*6. forbearance*
	7. forgiveness
	8. love

Helpful Hints for Christian Living (Col. 3:1–11):

1. *Seek those things which are above (3:1).*
2. *Set your mind on things above (3:2).*
3. *Put to death your past sins (3:5).*
4. *Be renewed in knowledge according to Him (3:10).*

LESSON EIGHT: DRESS FOR SUCCEESS

Spiritual Wardrobe (Col. 3:12-17):

1. *Tender mercies. Dorcas noticed the needs of those around her, made clothes for the widows, had compassion.*
2. *Kindness. Christians must be obedient and be a witness ("give no offense," verse 3).*
3. *Humility. Believer receives the kingdom of heaven, eternal life with the Father.*
4. *Meekness. The meek will inherit the earth, receive the power of God.*
5. *Longsuffering. The testing of your faith produces patience.*
6. *Tolerance. A gentle tongue is often needed to persuade a ruler.*
7. *Forgiveness. If believers do not forgive, the Father will not forgive us.*
8. *Love. When believers "put on love" they walk in love and obedience, are unselfish and kind to others.*

Wardrobe for Warfare (Eph. 6:13–18):
belt of truth (v.14)
breastplate of righteousness (v.14)
shoes of the gospel (v.15)
shield of faith (v.16)
helmet of salvation (v.17)
sword of the Spirit (v.17)

Biblical submission:
Willingly giving control of your life to someone in authority over you because of your love for the Lord.

Colossians 3:18–4:1:
Wives submit to husbands (v.18).
Husbands love wives (v. 19).
Children obey parents (v.20).
Fathers do not provoke children (v. 21).
Bondservants obey masters (v.22).
Masters be fair to servants (4:1).

How can fathers exasperate their children?
Ignoring them, being impatient with them, being too harsh, being critical.

Rewards of Submission:
1 Peter 3:1 - a vibrant witness
1 Peter 3:5–6 - glorify God
Ephesians 5:32,33 - teach spiritual truths
Titus 2:3-5 - train children
1 Peter 3:4 - increase worth
1 Peter 3:7 - build relationship with God

The believer's speech:
1 Corinthians 2:6–7 - speak wisdom
2 Corinthians 3:12 - speak truth
2 Corinthians 12:6 - speak of Christ
Ephesians 4:15 - speak and exhort (encourage)
Ephesians 5:32 - speak love

LESSON NINE: A SUBMISSIVE HEART

LESSON TEN: THE SPEECH OF A BELIEVER

Colossians 4:6 - speak boldly
Titus 2:15 - speak with grace

Colossians 4:2 - I must constantly, continually pray from my heart for myself and others, never forgetting to be thankful.

"Season speech with salt" (Col. 4:6)

The words of a Christian should cause thirst for God, plus encourage Christians to remain true to their faith (preservative), live holy lives (purifier), and experience Christian joy (flavoring).

1 Corinthians 3:18–4:5

Worldly Wisdom	Spiritual Wisdom
1. deceitful	1. true
2. foolish	2. wise
3. crafty	3. honest
4. futile	4. eternal
5. proud	5. humble
6. limited	6. unlimited
7. unjust	7. just
8. darkness	8. light
9. praise of man	9. praise of God

LESSON ELEVEN: A FOND FAREWELL

Purpose of the greeting in a New Testament letter:
To identify the author and extend expressions of love to and from others.

Did Paul accomplish the purpose of the greeting in Colossians?
Yes. In Colossians 1:1 he identified himself as author and in Colossians 4:10-14 he extended greetings from his companions to Christians in Colosse.

What is an epistle?
A biblical letter of instruction

Paul's blessings in his epistles:
Romans 16:24 - grace
1 Corinthians 16:23 - grace, love
2 Corinthians 13:14 - grace, love, communion

Galatians 6:18 - grace
Ephesians 6:24 - grace
Philippians 4:23 - grace
Colossians 4:18 - grace
1 Thessalonians 5:28 - grace
2 Thessalonians 3:18 - grace
1 Timothy 6:21 - grace
2 Timothy 4:22 - grace
Titus 3:15 - grace
Philemon 25 - grace

Emotions experienced by Paul (Col. 2:1-3):
- *concern, worry (v.1)*
- *love, care, compassion (v.2)*
- *unity, love (v.2)*

Human heresy:
man's perversion of truth for personal gain

Biblical truth:
God's unchangable, infallible Word for our good

How did Paul work (Col. 1:29)?
He labored long hours with great effort, striving dependently on God's power.

How should believers relate to other people (Col. 3:12–14)?
Believers should be merciful, kind, humble, meek, patient, tolerant, forgiving, and loving toward others.

What does scripture teach about spiritual wellness (Col. 2:6–7)?
If we walk in Him and stay rooted, and built up and established in Him we will not stumble. We will be spiritually well.

LESSON TWELVE:
FAITH AND
FITNESS
(CONCLUSION)

BIBLIOGRAPHY

Barclay, William, *The Letters to the Philippians, Colossians, and Thessalonians*, (Philadelphia: The Westminster Press, 1975).

Burroughs, Esther, *A Garden Path to Mentoring* (Birmingham: New Hope, 1997).

Butler, Trent C., gen. ed., *Holman Bible Dictionary* (Nashville: Holman Bible Publishers, 1991).

Cooper, Kenneth H., *It's Better to Believe: The New Medical Program that Uses Spiritual Motivation to Achieve Maximum Health and Add Years to Your Life* (Nashville: Thomas Nelson, 1995).

Dunnam, Maxie D., *The Communicator's Commentary: Galatians, Ephesians, Philippians, Colossians, Philemon* (Waco: Word Books, 1982).

Hendriksen, William, *New Testament Commentary: Colossians and Philemon* (Grand Rapids: Baker Book House, 1964).

MacArthur, John, Jr., *The MacArthur New Testament Commentary: Colossians and Philemon* (Chicago: Moody Press, 1992).

McGinn, Linda, *Equipped for Life: Ephesians, Philippians, Colossians* (Grand Rapids: Baker Books, 1994).

Mullins, E.Y., *Studies in Colossians* (Nashville: Sunday School Board of the Southern Baptist Convention, 1935).

Nelson's Complete Book of Bible Maps and Charts (Nashville: Thomas Nelson Publishers, 1993).

Severance, W. Murray, *Pronouncing Bible Names* (Nashville: Holman Bible Publishers, 1985).

Simpson, E.K. and F.F. Bruce, *The New International Commentary on the New Testament: Commentary on the Epistles to the Ephesians and Colossians* (Grand Rapids: Wm. B. Eerdmans Publishing, 1973).

Smith, Hannah Whitall, *The Christian's Secret to a Happy Life* (Westwood, NJ: Barbour and Company, 1985).

Smith, Pamela M, *Food for Life* (Lake Mary, FL: Creation House, 1994).

The Woman's Study Bible (Nashville: Thomas Nelson, 1995).

Wright, N. T., *Tyndale New Testament Commentaries: Colossians and Philemon* (Grand Rapids: Wm. B. Eerdmans Publishing Co., 1978).